"This book takes a clear, honest look at how your phobia is getting in the way of how you want to live your life. It offers supportive, sound advice on how to face your fears step-by-step, and gives readers the tools they need to overcome fears and phobias."

> —**Jennifer Shannon, MFT**, clinical director at the Santa Rosa Center for Cognitive-Behavioral Therapy, and author of *The Shyness and Social Anxiety Workbook for Teens*

"Andrea Umbach's terrific book takes the research-proven strategies of cognitive behavioral therapy and puts them at your fingertips. Easy-to-use forms and worksheets walk the reader, step-by-step, through the strategies for preparing and implementing an effective antiphobia action plan. I recommend this book for any young person with fears and phobias that get in the way of their life."

> —**Jonathan S. Abramowitz, PhD**, clinical psychologist and president of the Association for Behavioral and Cognitive Therapies, and author of *Getting Over OCD*

"Andrea Umbach has successfully crafted a guide to help teens address their anxiety. Based on cognitive behavioral principles, readers will undoubtedly benefit from the clearly described, pragmatic, and well-supported strategies contained within. There is no question that many young people will greatly benefit from reading this engaging text."

> —**Eric A. Storch, PhD**, professor and All Children's Hospital Guild Endowed Chair at the University of South Florida

"In *Conquer Your Fears and Phobias for Teens*, Andrea Umbach provides teens like yourself with a step-by-step guide for self-directed treatment for a wide range of anxiety-related problems. She'll walk you through the essential components of CBT, including exposure therapy, as well as thinking-related exercises that have also been proven effective. You may find that if you stick with the exercises in this book, you will reduce your anxiety and improve your quality of life. Of course, if you need professional help, you should absolutely get it. But even in that case, *Conquer Your Fears and Phobias for Teens* can be a great starting point and serve as a basis for your work with a therapist."

> —**David F. Tolin, PhD, ABPP**, director at the Anxiety Disorders Center at the Institute of Living, adjunct associate professor of psychiatry at the Yale School of Medicine, and author of *Face Your Fears*

"If you are a teenager wanting a straightforward way to challenge your anxiety—this book is for you. If you want to understand why your teen feels the way they feel—this book is for you. If [you are a professional who] treats teens with anxiety and want a guide to using cognitive behavioral therapy and exposure and response prevention—this book is for you. Read it, do the exercises, and watch your anxiety take a back seat in your life."

> —**Patrick B. McGrath, PhD**, clinical director at Alexian Brothers
> Behavioral Health Hospital's Center for Anxiety and Obsessive
> Compulsive Disorders

"Anxiety is all-around no fun. But backing away as comfort doesn't work much better. If you want help moving forward [from anxiety], this is your go-to guide. You'll be surprised at how quickly you can put fears and phobias in your rearview mirror as you drive toward your next adventure."

> —**Reid Wilson, PhD**, coauthor of *Anxious Kids, Anxious Parents* and
> *Playing with Anxiety*

"Reading this book is like having your own therapist for fears and phobias. It is crammed with information and lots of 'how-tos,' and manages to avoid the pitfalls of cookbook, manualized approaches. Most readers with fears and phobias will want to read sections over and over again, since there is too much information to absorb in one reading. Parents and therapists should find it a useful resource tool. This is a comprehensive, cutting-edge, third-wave, cognitive behavioral therapy (CBT) approach to [dealing with] fears and phobias, written in a style that will appeal to teenagers (for example, every quotation is from a contemporary character who should be well known by the target audience). I wish I had a resource like this when I was in my teens, struggling with my own anxieties."

> —**Martin N. Seif, PhD, ABPP**, clinical psychologist, founder of the
> Anxiety Disorders Association of America, associate director of the
> Anxiety and Phobia Treatment Center at White Plains Hospital,
> faculty member at New York Presbyterian Hospital, and coauthor
> of *What Every Therapist Needs to Know About Anxiety Disorders*

"Being afraid is part of the human condition, but when fear is overwhelming, life can be miserable. All of us, teens and adults, must learn to understand and manage our fears in order to lead happy and productive lives. *Conquer Your Fears and Phobias for Teens* is an essential guide to doing so. It provides a step-by-step program for recognizing, understanding, and controlling fears of all kinds. This long overdue book will provide much relief to teens and family members living with intense fears."

> —**Randy O. Frost, PhD**, author and coauthor of several books on hoarding, including *Buried in Treasures, Stuff: Compulsive Hoarding and the Meaning of Things, The Oxford Handbook of Hoarding and Acquiring,* and more

"The efficacy of Andrea Umbach's book comes in her ability to relate to teens on their level. For each clinical topic, she offers relatable examples in which teens will recognize themselves and their peers, thus dodging the eye roll and earning her way into their trust. From there, the exercises are easy, clear, and effective! Teens with fear, help is here."

> —**Michelle Icard**, author of *Middle School Makeover*

"*Conquering Your Fears and Phobias for Teens* is an engaging and practical guide for teens to overcome their fears. It is packed with clear, concise, and effective examples and exercises for teens, which will teach them invaluable life skills, helping them to think more flexibly, face their fears, and manage their anxiety more effectively. And it even cleverly addresses teens' common struggle with motivation and willingness. This reader-friendly workbook is the perfect fear-busting companion for teens and their parents and the therapists who wish to help them."

> —**Marla W. Deibler, PsyD**, clinical psychologist, founder and executive director of the Center for Emotional Health of Greater Philadelphia, and a nationally recognized expert in anxiety, obsessive compulsive, and related disorders, with appearances on *The Dr. Oz Show*, A&E's *Hoarders*, CBS News, ABC News, and FOX News

conquer your fears & phobias for teens

how to build courage & stop fear from holding you back

ANDREA UMBACH, PsyD

Instant Help Books
An Imprint of New Harbinger Publications, Inc.

Publisher's Note

This publication is designed to provide accurate and authoritative information in regard to the subject matter covered. It is sold with the understanding that the publisher is not engaged in rendering psychological, financial, legal, or other professional services. If expert assistance or counseling is needed, the services of a competent professional should be sought.

Distributed in Canada by Raincoast Books

Copyright © 2015 by Andrea Umbach
      Instant Help Books
      An Imprint of New Harbinger Publications, Inc.
      5674 Shattuck Avenue
      Oakland, CA 94609
      www.newharbinger.com

Cover design by Amy Shoup; Edited by Karen Schader; Acquired by Tesilya Hanauer

Library of Congress Cataloging-in-Publication Data on file

Printed in the United States of America

17   16   15

10   9   8   7   6   5   4   3   2   1   First printing

To my family for helping me believe I can do anything

To my husband for always encouraging me to face my fears

Contents

Acknowledgments

I would like to thank Linda Fama and Edward Shearin for their guidance and support when I first explored my interest in anxiety and cognitive behavioral therapy. I was very fortunate to have amazing supervisors and mentors early on who helped me find my path and passion. Charles Mansueto and colleagues at the Behavior Therapy Center of Greater Washington, I thank you for your dedication to your clients and your willingness to teach others. Your introduction to the anxiety community was invaluable. David Tolin and colleagues at the Anxiety Disorders Center, I thank you for your commitment to research and creative exposures. I sometimes miss sharing my office with a snake. To my new family at Southeast Psych, the amount of fun, innovation, and encouragement I experience on a daily basis is unending. I could not ask for better colleagues, mentors, and friends. Special thanks to Frank Gaskill, Dave Verhaagen, Jessica Bloomfield, Stephanie Kors, Rachel Maskin, Rachel Kitson, Austin Zoutewelle, Lauren King, Andrew King, and Zach Brown for your editing and contributions. Also, thank you to the staff at New Harbinger Publications for your diligence and suggestions. And last but definitely not least, thank you to those who have shared your greatest fears with me and allowed me to be a part of your journey.

Welcome

You can't let fear steal your funk.

—Marshall Eriksen in *How I Met Your Mother*

I'm so happy you decided to open this book. Since you're reading it, I'm guessing that you (or someone who cares about you) are concerned about your level of fear. Maybe there's one big thing that really scares you, or perhaps a lot of little things. Maybe you're overly cautious or you worry all the time. Whatever you fear, you are not alone. Everyone has fear. And millions (yes, millions) of teens struggle just like you to escape the power fear holds over their lives. So you've come to the right place.

There's work ahead and areas of your life to explore. This book will be your road map. Your destination is conquering your fear or phobia. In order to get there, you'll have to dig deep and really understand how fear has grabbed hold of you. You'll also need to think about the kind of life you really *want* to live.

With any journey, you'll have new experiences, come up against obstacles, and discover more about yourself. You can take this journey on your own, or you can share it with a parent, friend, or therapist. Most people find that support from others can be very helpful when they take on new challenges. Your journey may be exciting, exhausting, and even a little scary. But it will all be worth it when you can make important changes and live your life more freely.

If your fear or phobia is stopping you or slowing you down, then let's do something about it! Now is the time to conquer your fear or phobia. You really can do it.

Enjoy your adventure,

Dr. Andrea Umbach

Chapter 1

Healthy Fear vs. Hurtful Phobias

All creatures feel fear.

—Thomas Wayne in *Batman Begins*

Imagine it's a nice day and you decide to go outside and play basketball for a while. After ten minutes of practicing free throws, you decide to dribble around the block. You're about twenty feet from your driveway when you hear a dog barking. You suddenly realize the dog is running across the street and moving toward you. You get a quick glimpse and see it's your neighbor's Rottweiler. Without thinking, you drop the basketball and run as fast as you can to your front door. Once inside, you notice your heart is pounding and you're out of breath. But you're safe.

So what happened? Why were you scared? And how were you able to respond so quickly? The following section will help you better understand the nature of fear and how we react to fear.

We Want Fear!

Like joy, sadness, and anger, fear is a natural, basic human emotion. It's the intense feeling we experience when a situation appears to be dangerous or threatening. Although you may not think of fear as positive, it's actually a vital tool for survival. Fear alerts us to danger and helps us react in the moment so we can stay safe. In these examples of potentially dangerous situations, fear was actually the hero:

- Madison smelled smoke in her house and quickly ran outside and called 911.

- Shawn saw a box fall out of a truck on the highway and swerved out of the way.

- Olivia noticed a man following her in the park and decided to take a different route to be near other people.

- Tina knew there was a tornado headed for her city and went with her friends to a safety shelter.

- Zack heard a wolf howl near him while walking in the woods and decided to go back in the other direction.

- Sharon tipped her kayak on the river and quickly swam to shore.

While none of these people enjoyed being scared or wanted to be in these situations, their fear helped them act rapidly and get to safety.

List some threatening situations where fear has protected you:

_____

_____

_____

_____

Thankfully, you had your fear; otherwise you might not have made it through those situations. But you might be wondering, how is it that the human body reacts so quickly in threatening situations?

The answer is that fear is instinctual. We're born with survival instincts. Our bodies are programmed to respond automatically when we sense danger. In fact, our ancestors responded to the threats of wolves, bears, forest fires, and dangerous people hundreds of years ago in exactly the same way we respond to threats today.

Fear and Your Brain

Here comes your science lesson. It might sound boring, but hang in there—it gets pretty interesting. Your brain is very complex and has more than 100 billion neurons, firing about two hundred times per second. The neurons work together to create a highly effective communication system. When you're afraid, your brain's communication system is incredibly fast (we're talking milliseconds) and almost completely automatic.

You can compare your brain to a computer. It seems simple to operate—you just push a few buttons and it works. In reality, there's so much more going on. There are tons of wires, chips, and connected parts inside the computer that are all very important, but we don't really think about them. The computer is programmed to respond quickly and automatically without your having to give it hundreds of commands.

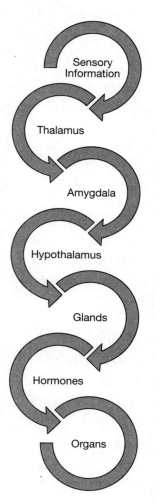

To help you better understand your fear reaction, let's look at the path fear takes through your brain and body. First, all incoming sensory information from your eyes, ears, mouth, and skin is sent instantly to a part of the brain called the thalamus. When you heard the dog barking and saw it was your neighbor's Rottweiler, this sensory information was sent to your thalamus.

You can think of the thalamus as a traffic controller because it decides where the information should go. However, it's hard for the thalamus to determine whether the situation is actually threatening. For example, *Is the dog coming to play with me or does it want to bite me?* To be safe, the thalamus sends the information to your amygdala. The amygdala receives the information and instinctually sends a distress signal to the hypothalamus.

The hypothalamus responds by hitting the "on switch," your sympathetic nervous system. This system mobilizes different parts of your body to respond to a threat. Basically, it prepares you to either fight against the threat or flee from it, which is known as your *fight-or-flight* response. The hypothalamus does this by sending nerve and chemical signals to glands in order to release hormones into your bloodstream. Finally, the hormones, such as adrenaline and cortisol, travel like little messengers through your blood to regulate the activities of the organs in your body.

To put it simply, your brain's fast communication with your sympathetic nervous system was responsible for increasing your heart rate and breathing in order to help you run away from the dog.

Fear and Your Body

So what effects do these hormones have on your body? What follows is a list of possible physical reactions in your body and a list of ways these physical reactions help your body fight against or protect yourself from danger. See if you can match each physical reaction with its purpose.

 This icon identifies a worksheet that can be downloaded at http://www .newharbinger.com/31458.

 This icon tells you to check the back of the book for sample responses or correct answers.

Physical Reaction

_____ 1. Heart rate increases

_____ 2. Breathing quickens

_____ 3. Blood sugar levels increase

_____ 4. Blood is redirected from skin, hands, and feet to larger muscles

_____ 5. Muscles tense

_____ 6. Sweat glands work harder

_____ 7. Activity in digestive system and salivary glands decreases

_____ 8. Pupils dilate

_____ 9. Attention increases

Purpose

a.   Takes in as much light as possible and increases visual field

b.   Keeps body cool and prevents overheating

c.   Provides more oxygen for muscles

d.   Prepares body for action with extra speed and strength

e.   Circulates oxygen-rich blood to cells and muscles more quickly

f.   Turns off unnecessary systems to direct energy to more important tasks

g.   Provides major muscles with more energy so they can respond quickly

h.   Gives energy boost

i.   Directs focus to threat and big picture

These physical reactions work together to give your body strength and speed to help you respond to a threatening situation. Fortunately, your body is designed to handle these kinds of reactions, so they're not at all harmful to you. You might even notice that you feel many of these same sensations when you exercise. Just remember, this is your body's natural and instinctual way of handling threatening situations and trying to keep you safe.

Your body cannot stay in this high alert and high-energy stage forever. When your fight-or-flight response runs its course or you receive some other information from the environment that you're no longer in danger, your brain will hit the "off switch," your parasympathetic nervous system, and your body will begin to return to its normal state. It may take some time for all the hormones to return to normal levels, which is why it may take a little while for all your symptoms to go away completely. Also, because the fight-or-flight response requires so much energy, you'll usually feel tired after such an event.

Everyone Has Fear

Hopefully from this discussion, you recognize these points:

- Fear is a basic emotion.

- Fear triggers natural and instinctual reactions in your body.

- We all need fear in order to protect ourselves from danger.

We even expect children to have certain fears when they are young. Common childhood fears include fear of the dark, water, ghosts, monsters, strangers, or of being alone. Fear is actually protective as children cautiously explore new and unfamiliar environments. But as children learn more about their environment, they are generally able to navigate these situations without having their fear responses triggered. This means they're able to outgrow some early fears as their brains develop and they have more experiences.

What childhood fears did you have that you were able to outgrow? If you aren't sure, ask someone who knew you well as a child.

_____

_____

_____

Even though we outgrow some fears, everyone still has fear. Think about how many adults would experience fear if they were in a car accident or an earthquake. They would definitely be scared. Even the strongest, toughest people you know have fears, whether they would be willing to admit it or not.

When Is Fear Hurtful?

Have you ever heard the phrase "too much of a good thing"? Think about the things in life that are really great but become problematic if we have an excess of them. Look at this list of items people usually enjoy—adding any items you feel are missing from the list in the lines provided—and determine what the unfortunate consequences might be if we have too much.

- Too much food =

- Too much sun =

- Too much exercise =

- Too much money =

- Too much time with one friend =

- Too much alcohol =

- Too much work =

- Too many possessions =

- Too many activities =

- _____

- _____

What about the phrase "everything in moderation"? Way back in 1908, researchers realized that we function and perform best under moderate levels of arousal or stimulation. With too little stimulation, we're unmotivated, bored, unproductive, and careless. With too much stimulation, we're overwhelmed, stressed, exhausted, and burned out. Ultimately, we want to be somewhere in the middle, where we're motivated, energized, and productive.

Think about how that concept relates to your fear:

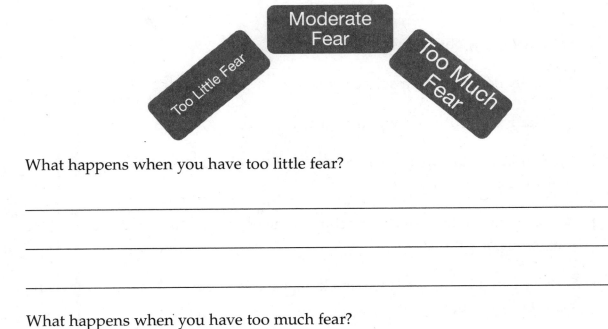

What happens when you have too little fear?

_____

_____

_____

What happens when you have too much fear?

_____

_____

_____

What happens when you have moderate fear?

_____

_____

_____

What Exactly Is a Phobia?

Since you're reading this book, you probably have more fear in your life than you would like. It's possible you have something called a phobia. "Phobia" is actually the Greek word for fear. A phobia is also thought of as a type of anxiety. The list below describes some of the characteristics of phobias. Check the ones you think apply to you.

☐ I fear a specific object or situation.

☐ I'm really bothered or upset by my fear.

☐ My fear is stubborn and will not go away.

☐ My fear becomes stronger when I get near the object or situation, or know I will soon be.

☐ My body has an intense fear reaction to the object or situation, as if it's dangerous or a threat.

☐ I worry about losing control, panicking, or feeling physical symptoms when near the object or situation.

☐ I do everything I can to stay away from the object or situation.

☐ I tolerate the object or situation when I have to, but I'm very uncomfortable.

☐ When I'm away from the object or situation, I realize my fear is excessive or silly, or that it doesn't make sense.

☐ My fear, reactions, or avoidance of the object or situation greatly interferes with my daily routine, academics, or social life.

Phobias are not a sign of weakness. They can be thought of as fears that have gotten out of control or become too big, like a snowball rolling downhill and gathering more snow as it goes.

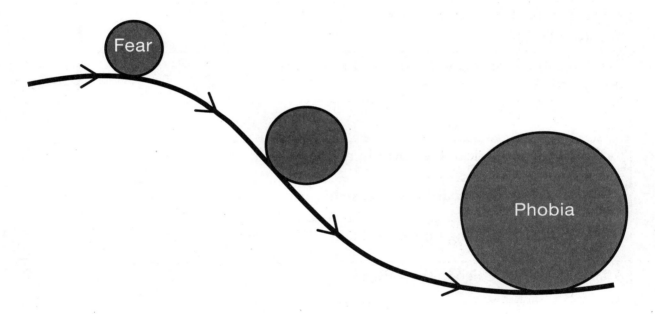

However, phobias have little to do with real danger; instead, they are false alarms. The amygdala sends out distress signals when there is actually no danger. But the danger feels real because your body reacts to real alarms and false alarms in the same way. Basically, your amygdala is getting triggered and activating the rest of your body when the situation does not actually require it.

You can use the question "bear or squirrel?" to help you recognize the difference between real threats and false alarms. If you're walking through the woods and hear rustling in the bushes, and a grizzly bear walks out, this would definitely be a real threat. If you hear the same sounds and a squirrel runs out, this would be a false alarm. In both situations your fear is triggered, but it's necessary for survival only with the bear.

Real Threat vs. False Alarm

See if you can tell the difference between real threats and false alarms. Remember that real threats require an immediate reaction in order to keep you safe. False alarms may seem scary, but in reality there is no immediate danger.

Situation	Real Threat (Bear)	False Alarm (Squirrel)
A bat is flying around Mia's house and might have already bitten her.		
Kristi is eating greasy food and feels like she might throw up.		
An ant crawls onto Mark's arm.		
Jorden sees an electrical line down in her front yard.		
Trey falls off his skateboard and breaks his arm.		
Sasha is afraid of getting into an accident while driving.		
An older boy hits Caleb in the hallway.		
Jacob gets a head rush when he goes down the waterslide.		
Josh's friend shows him his loaded gun.		
Ella is choking on a piece of food.		
Craig thinks the elevator might get stuck.		
Tammy hates getting shots, and it's time for her flu shot.		

How Common Are Phobias?

The good news is that you are definitely not alone. In 2005, researchers surveyed 9,282 adults in the United States and found that 28.8% of adults have had an anxiety disorder in their lifetime. Even more interesting, phobias were the most common type of anxiety disorder, with 12.5% of anxious adults having a specific phobia and 12.1% having a social phobia. Phobias are even more common than problems you might hear about more frequently, like obsessive-compulsive disorder (1.6%) or post-traumatic stress disorder (6.8%).

In 2010, researchers surveyed 10,123 teens in the United States. They found that 31.9% of teens have had an anxiety disorder in their lifetime. Once again, phobias were the most common type of anxiety disorder, with 19.3% of anxious teens having a specific phobia and 9.1% having a social phobia. This study also found that all anxiety disorders, including phobias, were more frequent in female teens.

So let's think about this in numbers that might make a little more sense. Let's estimate that an average high school grade has 100 students in it and the whole high school has about 400 students. This means about 19 other teens in your grade and 76 other teens in your high school are likely to be struggling with phobias. Overall, there are about 128 students in the school who are dealing with anxiety issues.

Sometimes people dealing with fears and phobias feel very alone and believe they are the only ones with these types of issues. Remember, no one is perfect. We all have something we're trying to work on, even if the people around us are not aware of it. While one person might be struggling with math, others might be working on their organization skills or their attitude. Think about your friends and family members. What problems might they be struggling with and trying to work on?

_____

_____

_____

_____

Phobias Among the Famous

Remember, anyone can have a phobia. It does not mean they have done anything wrong, they are weak, or something is wrong with them. Check out the following list of celebrities who have described what could be their own phobias:

- Oprah Winfrey: Fear of gum chewing

- Madonna: Fear of thunder

- Daniel Radcliffe and Johnny Depp: Fear of clowns

- Justin Timberlake: Fear of spiders

- Orlando Bloom: Fear of pigs

- Matthew McConaughey: Fear of tunnels and revolving doors

- Jennifer Love Hewitt: Fear of the dark and elevators

- David Beckham: Fear of untidiness

- Christina Ricci: Fear of houseplants

- Kelly Osbourne: Fear of being touched

- Nicole Kidman: Fear of butterflies

- Scarlett Johansson: Fear of cockroaches

- Adele: Fear of seagulls

- Rihanna: Fear of fish or sea creatures

- Sheryl Crow and Tobey Maguire: Fear of heights

- Tom Cruise: Fear of going bald

- Jennifer Aniston and Whoopi Goldberg: Fear of flying

- Hugh Jackman: Fear of dolls

- Billy Bob Thornton: Fear of antique furniture

- Britney Spears: Fear of reptiles

- Hilary Duff: Fear of dirt

- Kristen Wiig: Fear of blood

- Keanu Reeves: Fear of darkness

- Lyle Lovett: Fear of cows

- Michael Jackson: Fear of contamination and infections

- George Washington and Edgar Allan Poe: Fear of being buried alive

- Richard Nixon: Fear of hospitals

Types of Phobias

As you can see, there are many different types of phobias. The content of a phobia can be just about anything. But remember, in order to be considered a phobia, it must cause someone distress and really affect important areas of life. This list gives you some more examples of phobias and their interesting names:

- Aloneness: monophobia or autophobia

- Animals: zoophobia

- Anything new: neophobia

- Bacteria: bacteriophobia

- Bees: apiphobia or melissophobia

- Being touched: aphenphosmphobia, haptephobia, or chiraptophobia

- Birds: ornithophobia

- Blood: hemophobia or hematophobia

- Bridges (or of crossing them): gephyrophobia

- Cats: ailurophobia, felinophobia, or gatophobia

- Cemeteries: coimetrophobia

- Children: pedophobia

- Choking: anginophobia

- Clowns: coulrophobia

- Colors: chromophobia or chromatophobia

- Confined spaces: claustrophobia

- Contamination with dirt or germs: bacteriophobia or mysophobia

- Crossing streets: agyrophobia or dromophobia

- Crowded public places: agoraphobia

- Darkness: achluophobia, nyctophobia, or scotophobia

- Death or dying: thanatophobia

- Decisions: decidophobia

- Demons: demonophobia or daemonophobia

- Dentists: dentophobia or odontophobia

- Disorder or untidiness: ataxophobia

- Dogs: cynophobia

- Fainting: asthenophobia

- Fire: arsonphobia or pyrophobia

- Flying: aviophobia or aviatophobia

- Forests or wooden objects: xylophobia

- Friday the Thirteenth: paraskavedekatriaphobia

- Ghosts: phasmophobia

- Heights: acrophobia or altophobia

- Hospitals: nosocomephobia

- Imperfection: atelophobia

- Injury: traumatophobia

- Insects: entomophobia or insectophobia

- Lightning and thunder: brontophobia or keraunophobia

- Loud noises: ligyrophobia or phonophobia

- Medicine: pharmacophobia

- Needles or sharp objects: aichmophobia or belonephobia

- Oceans: thalassophobia

- Reptiles: herpetophobia

- Riding in cars: amaxophobia or motorphobia

- Snakes: ophidiophobia or snakephobia

- Spiders: arachnephobia or arachnophobia

- The number 13: triskaidekaphobia

- 666: hexakosioihexekontahexaphobia

- Vomiting: emetophobia

- Water: hydrophobia

- Weight gain: obesophobia or pocrescophobia

The most commonly diagnosed phobias fall into six categories. It's also possible for someone to experience more than one phobia from the same or different categories.

- Animal phobias: dogs, cats, mice, birds, snakes, insects, spiders, and more

- Natural environment phobias: heights, darkness, water, storms

- Situational phobias: driving, flying, elevators, tunnels, bridges, crowded spaces, closed-in spaces

- Blood, injection, or injury phobias: seeing blood or injury, doctors, dentists

- Social phobias: performing, speaking in public, talking to unfamiliar people, other situations having a possibility of judgment or embarrassment

- Other phobias: vomiting, choking, contracting illness, getting hurt, gaining weight, loud noises, foods, clowns

Use the chart below to collect some information about your phobias. You might need to do some investigating or googling to find all the information:

Phobia	Technical Name	Category	Someone Else Who Has This Phobia
Example: *I'm afraid of high places.*	*Acrophobia*	*Natural environment*	*Sheryl Crow, my mom, and my friend Mary*

Now that you understand the difference between helpful fear and hurtful phobias, you can practice applying this information to your everyday life. Think about how your brain and body respond to fear in order to protect you in dangerous situations, and remember that the same response can also be triggered in false-alarm situations. If you think you have too much fear, resulting in a phobia, then you're reading the right book. Just like millions of other people, you have a fear that just wants to stick around. In chapters 2 and 3, you'll learn about where your phobias might have come from and why some fears are hard to outgrow.

Chapter 2

Where Did Your Phobia Come From?

We can't choose where we come from but we can choose where we go from there. I know it's not all the answers but it was enough to start putting these pieces together.

—Charlie in *The Perks of Being a Wallflower*

When we're struggling with problems, we tend to ask ourselves a lot of questions: *Why did this happen to me? What's wrong with me? Where did this come from?* It can be very frustrating when we don't know the cause of our problems. But there is good news! Scientists and researchers have spent years trying to figure out how phobias start in the first place. In this chapter, you'll be able to investigate the possible roots of your phobia. Most often, there isn't one simple answer, and we have to take our best guesses at what factors might contribute to our phobias. Fortunately, guessing is good enough because we don't need to know the exact cause of the phobia in order to overcome it. So let's see what we can dig up!

What Did You Inherit?

DNA is in every cell in the human body and contains the biological instructions for our development. Short segments of DNA are called genes. Every person has about 20,000 genes, which help determine traits such as your eye color, hair type, blood type, and even whether you can curl your tongue. Genes are packed tightly together to form two sets of twenty-three chromosomes. One set of chromosomes comes from your mother and the other from your father.

If you think of a chromosome as a playlist, then genes are like songs. The twenty-three playlists you got from your mom and the twenty-three you got from your dad are different from what your siblings got. And that is what makes you unique.

This means you can thank your parents for all the great traits they gave you, like your intelligence, good looks, or sparkling personality. You may also have some traits from your parents you aren't so excited about. Maybe you have your dad's crooked toes or your mom's asthma. Whatever it is, it isn't anyone's fault. It's just the way your genes randomly came together.

So what might you inherit from your parents that would result in a phobia? This is where scientists aren't exactly sure, but they have a few guesses. What we do know is that anxiety tends to run in families. Researchers like to study twins because they can compare identical twins (the twins you can't tell apart), who have 100 percent of the same genetic makeup, to fraternal twins (the twins who look different or are even different genders), who have 50 percent of the same genetic makeup. This comparison helps them distinguish how much a symptom is related to genetic factors versus environmental factors (which will be explained more later). Ultimately, many studies of families and twins have shown that if you have a close relative with anxiety or a phobia, you're more likely to have anxiety or a phobia.

What researchers don't know is *what* exactly is inherited. Perhaps you inherited a certain personality type that is a little more sensitive, reactive, or prone to anxiety and fear. Or you could have inherited low levels of neurotransmitters that regulate your amygdala (the part that sends the distress signal). Or your sympathetic nervous system might be more excitable. Thankfully, even if you inherited some of these things, there are still ways to conquer your phobia.

Think about your family members. Do your parents or any close family members have a phobia? Do they seem to get nervous or anxious a lot?

_____

_____

_____

_____

When Did You Connect the Dots?

Not all phobias are inherited. There are many examples of teens who have phobias and their family members don't. So there must be something else going on, right? Researchers such as physiologist Ivan Pavlov and psychologists John Watson and Stanley Rachman suggested that learning and making associations is the answer.

Back in 1901, Pavlov was the first to discover learned associations. Have you ever heard of his famous dog experiments? Pavlov noticed that dogs could make a connection between a sound and their food. This sound hadn't meant anything to the dogs until food was involved. When Pavlov purposely rang a bell at feeding time, it became a cue, and soon the dogs began to salivate whenever they heard the bell. A connection was made: bell meant food. From this, Pavlov believed that when two things happen together or right after another repeatedly, we tend to associate the two and expect one when we have the other.

Years later, Watson used the idea of learned associations to explore how phobias were developed. He played with a nine-month-old boy called Little Albert to see what would scare him. Sounds mean, right? Well, what he observed was very interesting. Little Albert showed no fear when he was first exposed to a rat, rabbit, monkey, mask, and burning newspaper. But later, Watson had Little Albert play with the rat, and he purposefully made a very loud noise, which startled Little Albert and made him cry. Watson did this several times (which wasn't very nice). Then Little Albert became frightened and upset when he saw the rat even without the loud noise. Even worse, he became afraid of anything that was furry and resembled the rat. When we fear objects similar to the original feared object, we are generalizing. Ultimately, Watson proved that connecting an object that was once harmless and enjoyable (the rat) with something disturbing (the noise) resulted in a phobia.

More recently, Rachman suggested that phobias are created when someone has a direct, negative experience with an object or a situation. For example:

- Since Brianna was stuck in a broken elevator for two hours, she becomes scared when she needs to use an elevator.

- When he was ice fishing, Paul fell through the ice and now fears lakes and large bodies of water.

- Jamie's first shot was very painful and scary, and now she hates all doctors.

- When eating dinner at her friend's cabin, Kelly choked on a fishbone. She refuses to eat any seafood or meat products.

- Cole threw up after a spinning carnival ride and now fears all carnival and park rides.

- Liza passed out from dehydration during a 5K race and is afraid to exercise now.

In each of these situations, something uncomfortable or bad happened, and the people associated their negative experiences with particular objects or situations. They decided the object or situation would always be dangerous and threatening, even though that might not actually be the case. While people can have similar negative experiences, only some develop phobias based on their associations at that time. These associations can be made after one really uncomfortable experience or several less severe experiences.

Think about what negative experiences in your past might be connected to your current phobia. What associations have you made?

_____

_____

_____

_____

_____

It's okay if you can't remember or can't think of anything. It's possible it was something small or subtle, or maybe this type of association isn't part of the picture. Keep reading to find out about more possibilities.

What Have You Observed?

Take a minute to think about how you learn to do things. Maybe you teach yourself by trying things out and learning from your mistakes. Or maybe you read a book about it and study really hard. But you probably learn most things by watching other people. Think back. How did you learn to walk or write? To ride a bike? To do math problems or use a computer? To cook a meal?

Did you teach yourself all these things, or did you learn by watching someone else do them first? If you think back far enough, you might realize that one of the first steps was watching someone else, even if you didn't realize you were doing it. We learn from examples, or what we sometimes call modeling. We learn from parents, siblings, teachers, friends, and even people on TV. They show us how to do things so we don't have to figure it all out on our own. We rely on other people's wisdom and experience to lead us in the right direction.

What are other examples of useful things you've learned by observing others?

_____

_____

_____

Unfortunately, in the same way we learn how to do really cool and helpful things, we can also learn how to do some not-so-great things. For example:

- Tanya watched her older sister steal candy at the gas station. She started to do it too, but ended up getting caught.

- Graham heard his friends teasing a younger boy at lunch, and he started joining in so he would fit in.

- Juliet watched her mother throw trash on the ground when they were walking around town. Now she thinks littering isn't a big deal because everyone does it.

- Kelsey saw a TV show where a girl sneaked out of her house to hang out with friends. She tried it and it didn't go exactly as well as it did on TV.

Another unfortunate possibility is learning how to do something wrong by watching others. For example:

- Mary's friend showed her how to change the oil in her car, but her friend didn't really know how to do it and damaged the car.

- Tim wanted to learn how to head a soccer ball. He watched his coach head the ball, but unfortunately, the coach was doing it wrong.

- Alexis helped her friend make cookies for her birthday, but the cookies didn't end up tasting very good. When she tried making them on her own, she realized her friend hadn't followed the recipe correctly.

- Lauren's dad always made it a point to teach her how to use her money wisely. But without intending to, he taught her to underpay waiters because he didn't calculate tips accurately.

You get the idea. Sometimes learning from others doesn't go so well, and it might happen more often than we realize. What are some examples of negative things you've learned from others? When have you learned something unhelpful or not entirely accurate from others?

_____

_____

_____

_____

So what does learning have to do with phobias? You've probably guessed that you can learn to be phobic by watching others being phobic. If you see that someone else is really afraid of something, you might learn to be afraid of it too. You may even become afraid of an object or situation without actually experiencing it yourself. Also, you might start to react in a certain way because you watched how someone else was reacting.

When Cassie was growing up, she often saw her mother start to breathe heavily and shake in any situation involving heights. As a young child, without even realizing it, Cassie learned that heights were bad and scary. Since her mother tried to avoid anything that had to do with heights, Cassie started to avoid them as well. She specifically remembers when her class went on a trip to Washington, DC, and her mother had a panic attack at the Washington Monument. Cassie also refused to go anywhere near the monument. Cassie learned to be afraid of heights by observing her mother's reactions.

If you see someone else hurt or in pain, you might also learn to be afraid.

Dan was very close with his grandfather, who had become very ill when Dan was ten. Since he enjoyed visiting his grandfather every Sunday afternoon, Dan's mother agreed they would visit, but only for short periods of time. Dan could see that his grandfather was really struggling. On one occasion, his grandfather was very tired and coughing heavily. On another, he was in the bathroom throwing up. But worst of all was the day Dan's grandfather coughed and blood came out of his mouth. Dan became very scared. He started to believe that if he coughed he might throw up or cough up blood as well. He also started to avoid things that he thought might make him sick. He refused to touch doorknobs others had touched and skipped school when a classmate had a cold. Even though Dan was not sick, he was always afraid he might be.

These examples show us that sometimes our phobias have to do with what we observe, not necessarily what we experience ourselves. What observations might have played a role in your phobia?

_____

_____

_____

_____

What Have You Heard?

There are thousands of media sources in the world. Think of all the different places where you can get information: TV, radio, billboards, magazines, and the Internet. Oh, and there are still newspapers and books around too. People like to be informed, and with all our technology, we hear about things really quickly. So how does this affect our lives?

We're constantly bombarded by messages. We would like to think we're getting a good balance of both positive and negative messages in the media, but the reality is that the bad news usually far outweighs the good news. Think about it: when you turn on the news, are you more likely to hear about children raising money for charity or about a tragic accident? Unfortunately, the media often uses fear in order to get the audience's attention. Since everyday things are not very exciting, what is usually reported are the exceptions to the rule, rare circumstances, and exaggerated consequences. This leaves viewers and readers feeling unsafe and scared.

As a result, the information we receive also contributes to phobias. People can have no contact at all with an object or situation (not experiencing it personally or observing it), yet become afraid of it. Warnings and cautions alone can create fear. For example:

- Liam heard about a "sea monster" found in California and is afraid to go into any body of water.

- Kara saw a picture in the newspaper of a tornado that destroyed many homes in another state, and now she refuses to go outside.

- Jayden saw a TV news report about food poisoning at a local restaurant and will no longer eat out.

- Jessica watched a video on YouTube about someone being attacked and injured by a dog, and now she's afraid of all dogs.

We also get information from people we know: our parents, teachers, and friends. In most cases, people who are close to us are just trying to give us helpful warnings so we can stay safe. However, sometimes they can exaggerate, especially if they have their own phobias and anxiety. For example:

- Molly's mom told her never to go to the mall without an adult because someone could try to kidnap her. Now she is afraid to be alone anywhere.

- Robert's teacher has repeatedly warned the class about playing too many video games. He explained that video games make kids violent and ruin their vision. Now Robert is afraid to play them at all.

- Kevin's friend told him the lady next door practices black magic and puts curses on people. Now he is afraid of his neighbor and stays as far away from her house as possible.

- Christina's sister told her that if she doesn't get enough sleep, she'll die. Now Christina worries excessively about getting the right amount of sleep and panics if she can't fall asleep at the right time.

While some of the warnings we get from people are both necessary and appropriate, we have to watch out for the ones that seem exaggerated or unrealistic. In Molly's case, she should be careful when going to the mall, but she doesn't need to avoid being alone altogether. In Robert's, Kevin's, and Christina's cases, they received inaccurate or exaggerated information, which caused them to exaggerate their own behaviors as a result. Although the situations described in the warnings seemed scary, we know they are not necessarily true. This doesn't mean you don't have to listen to your parents, but it does mean you have to think critically about the warnings and information you're hearing. We'll discuss this more in chapter 6.

What information have you heard about your phobic object or situation? Where did you hear it?

_____

_____

_____

_____

Other Factors to Consider

Some other areas that might contribute to your phobia include experience and life stress. The amount of experience you have with a certain object or situation might determine how you respond to it. Let's use snakes as an example:

Anne loves snakes and owns three as pets. She cares for them, feeds them, and even lets them hang around her neck.

Dominique has no experience with snakes. She has seen them on TV and in books a few times, but never in real life.

Imagine that both Anne and Dominique had the unfortunate experience of being bitten by a snake today. Do you think that they would both develop phobias as a result?

What would happen to Anne? Why?

_____

_____

What would happen to Dominique? Why?

_____

_____

Since there are many other factors involved, we don't know for sure, but we can take a guess. It's likely that Anne won't develop a phobia because she has a lot of knowledge about snakes, she cares about them, and she has had many positive experiences with them to outweigh this one negative experience. Dominique, however, might develop a phobia because her one and only experience with snakes was a bad one. Without any experience to convince her that snakes might not be threatening, she'll probably want to stay away from them.

How much experience did you have with your phobic object or situation before your phobia started? Did you have enough positive experiences to outweigh a negative experience?

_____

_____

_____

_____

Another area to consider is the amount of stress in your life. We all have stressful situations in our lives. To be honest, stress is not always a bad thing. It often keeps us moving and being productive. But if we have too much stress or don't handle it in the right way, it may start to affect other areas of our lives.

Melissa moved for the fifth time to a new town and new school. Her parents are getting a divorce, and her grandmother passed away two weeks ago. She is having a hard time keeping up in school and is struggling to make new friends.

Lee is studying for his midterm exams and feels pressure to get good grades. He also has a huge state wrestling championship coming up next week. Lee is conflicted about how to split his time between school, wrestling, and being with friends. But he has felt this way before and knows he'll be able to get everything done.

Imagine that both Melissa and Lee were visiting a large city during a school break. Downtown was crazy busy, they were separated from their parents, and their cell phone batteries were dead. What do you think would happen next? Would they both develop phobias because they were overwhelmed and lost?

What would happen to Melissa? Why?

_____

_____

What would happen to Lee? Why?

_____

_____

As you probably guessed, Melissa is more likely to develop a phobia than Lee is. She has been through many stressful situations recently and is having a hard time. She probably doesn't have the energy or confidence to get herself through another difficult situation right now. It's also likely that getting lost is a much more negative experience for her than it is for Lee because of all her stress. Lee, on the other hand, probably has a better chance of getting through this situation without any long-term negative consequences. He might get overwhelmed but likely has the mental resources and ability to recover quickly.

How much stress do you have in your life? Does it feel like a manageable amount or are you extremely overwhelmed by it?

_____

_____

_____

What was your stress level like when your phobia started? Could stress have affected the onset of your phobia?

_____

_____

_____

Putting the Pieces Together

Now that you know about some of the factors that can lead to phobias, see if you can figure out the possible causes for these teens.

Betsy just completed the classroom portion of driver's education and is required to practice thirty hours of driving with one parent in the car. She's never driven before and is very fearful. Her father has offered to help her practice since she thinks her mother would just make her more nervous. Betsy's mother is a very cautious driver and told Betsy to look for an exit strategy at all times, specifically staying in the right lane as much as possible for an easy escape. Even when her father drives, her mother is constantly telling him how to drive and holding on tight. Also, Betsy's driver's education teacher made things even worse when he repeatedly emphasized teen accident and death rates. Betsy has been in only one car accident when she was young and doesn't remember it very well. However, last year, two girls from her school were riding a scooter and were hit by a car. This was the first funeral Betsy had ever attended.

What might have caused Betsy's driving phobia? Fill in the information you learned about Betsy. Remember, she may or may not be affected by all the factors listed.

Possible Factors	Betsy's Phobia Factors
Genetically inherited	
Direct negative association	
Observation and learning	
Information	
Amount of experience	
Level of stress	

For the last month, Alex has been sleeping on the couch in the living room. When his parents first noticed, they thought he was sneaking downstairs at night to watch TV, but then they realized he didn't want to sleep in his bedroom. Alex used to love his room, so they were confused. They knew that the biggest change in Alex's life had been his brother's birth and thought the baby's crying in the room next to his might be part of the problem. One day, Alex finally confessed that he had watched a scary movie at his friend's house, and since then he'd been afraid of the dark. He had kept the light on by his bed for several nights, but he was still scared. He knew it was just a movie, but when he turned off the lights, he thought he heard things moving around in his room. Then, when doing research on famous pilots for a school project, Alex learned about Charles Lindbergh, whose baby was kidnapped in 1932. Alex didn't want to sleep in his room alone, so he decided to sleep on the couch closer to his parents' room, with light from the TV.

What might have caused Alex's phobia of the dark and his bedroom? Fill in the information you learned about Alex. Remember, he may or may not be affected by all the factors listed.

Possible Factors	Alex's Phobia Factors
Genetically inherited	
Direct negative association	
Observation and learning	
Information	
Amount of experience	
Level of stress	

What Are Your Phobia Factors?

Now it's your turn to put the pieces together. Go back and look at your answers to the questions in the chapter to help you fill out your phobia factors. Remember, you might not have every factor listed.

Possible Factors	My Phobia Factors
Genetically inherited • Do your parents or any close family members have a phobia? • Do they seem to get nervous or anxious a lot?	
Direct negative association • What negative experiences in your past might be connected to your phobia? • What associations have you made?	
Observation and learning • What observations might have played a role in your phobia? • What have you learned from others in relation to your phobia?	
Information • What information have you heard about your phobic object or situation? • Where did you hear it?	
Amount of experience • How much experience did you have with your phobic object or situation before your phobia started? • Did you have enough positive experiences to outweigh a negative experience?	
Level of stress • What was your stress level like when your phobia started? • Could stress have affected the onset of your phobia?	

Now we're going to create a timeline of your phobia to help you see the way it has developed. Let's use Alex as an example. Each dot on the timeline shown represents an event or factor in Alex's life that may have influenced his phobia. The curved line marks the strength of his phobia, showing when it started and how it became more extreme over time.

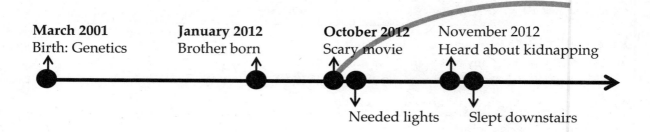

March 2001
Birth: Genetics

January 2012
Brother born

October 2012
Scary movie

November 2012
Heard about kidnapping

Needed lights   Slept downstairs

Here are some possible events or factors for your timeline:

- The first time I remember being afraid of my phobia

- Specific situations that triggered my phobia

- Times I observed something that triggered my phobia

- Times I heard information related to my phobia

- Specific situations that made my phobia worse (like stressful events)

What is your phobia timeline?

Birth:

Once you've plotted the factors on your timeline, with a different color pen or pencil, draw a line to show the strength of your phobia throughout your life. Notice whether it stayed the same once it started, or got better or worse.

Hopefully this chapter helped you understand the possible roots of your phobia. Remember, your phobia might be related to one factor or many different factors working together. And maybe you still don't know for sure but can take a good guess about what might have happened. Either way, the next step is to understand not only what might have started your phobia but also what has kept it going for so long or even made it worse. The next chapter will help you explore the spiraling phobia pattern.

Chapter 3

What Keeps Your Phobia Alive?

Understanding is the first step to acceptance,
and only with acceptance can there be recovery.

—Albus Dumbledore in *Harry Potter and the Goblet of Fire*

In the last chapter, you were able to explore the possible causes of your phobia. While this might be interesting, the factors that caused the phobia might have happened years ago, and it's actually more important to know why your phobia keeps hanging around. So let's focus on what's happening now and figure out what keeps your phobia going.

Looking for Patterns

Patterns are everywhere. We see them in nature, art, math, clothing, architecture, and more. A pattern is basically anything that repeats itself in a predictable way. It gives you a pretty good idea about what might come next based on what you already know or see. Let's look at a few patterns:

In each of these patterns, you can probably guess what might be coming next.

While these examples are visual, we also repeat patterns in nonvisual ways. Think about the way you do certain activities or routines. Sometimes when we figure out how to do something, we repeat it the same way. For example, athletes try very hard to repeat the same body motion over and over to produce positive results. Some people use the same morning routine every day so they don't forget a step. We even repeat patterns in video games, using certain button combinations to help us with moves.

What patterns or routines do you notice in your life?

_____

_____

_____

We also use a very basic psychological pattern all the time without really thinking about it. When we find ourselves in any type of situation, we think, feel, and act. This pattern is going on constantly. For example:

Cory wakes up in the morning and walks downstairs for breakfast. He thinks about what he wants for breakfast and decides on eggs. His stomach starts to growl, and he begins to salivate. He takes the ingredients out of the refrigerator to cook.

Parts of the Pattern	Cory's Pattern
Situation	Breakfast
Thoughts	What do I want for breakfast? Eggs
Emotion or physical sensations	Growling stomach and salivation
Action	Getting eggs out to cook

Got the pattern? How about this situation?

Tyson is working on a paper for school, and his little brother Tim keeps coming into his room. Tim wants to play basketball and is bouncing the ball in Tyson's room. Tyson thinks about how annoying Tim is and that he needs to get his work done. He starts to get frustrated. Then he remembers his brother still owes him ten dollars. Now he's really angry. Tyson pushes Tim into the hallway, slams the door, and yells at Tim to leave him alone forever.

Parts of the Pattern	Tyson's Pattern
Situation	Working on my paper and Tim comes in
Thoughts	Tim is annoying; I need to get this done
Emotion or physical sensations	Frustration, pressure
Thoughts	Tim owes me money
Emotion or physical sensations	Anger
Action	Pushing, slamming door, and yelling

As you can see in Tyson's example, sometimes we have lots of thoughts and emotions. Thoughts and emotions tend to influence each other and ultimately determine what action we take. You can also see that this pattern occurs in both positive and negative situations. At times, it can be really hard to pick out each part of the pattern because it happens so fast. It also might be difficult to notice what is happening in the moment, but if we look back and think about it, we can usually find the pattern.

Thought or Emotion?

Distinguishing thoughts from emotions can be really challenging. For example, how many times have you heard people say they *feel* like someone does not like them? This is actually a thought, not an emotion. Think of emotions as your mood or how you experience situations, rather than what is simply running through your head at the time.

Here is a list of emotions grouped with similar types of emotions. Add any you think may be missing.

- Happy: joyful, excited, enthusiastic, encouraged, optimistic

- Love: attracted, caring, compassionate, accepted

- Surprised: amazed, curious

- Confident: secure, proud, capable

- Relieved: content, satisfied, calm

- Sad: unhappy, down, depressed, lonely

- Hopeless: discouraged, pessimistic, defeated

- Inferior: worthless, inadequate, defective, insecure, rejected

- Disappointed: let down

- Embarrassed: foolish, humiliated, self-conscious

- Anxious: worried, panicky, nervous, on-edge, apprehensive

- Fearful: frightened, scared, shocked

- Frustrated: stuck, confused, lost

- Angry: mad, annoyed, irritated, upset, agitated, full of rage

- Ashamed: guilty, regretful, remorseful

- Jealous: envious

- _____

- _____

Try to decide which of the following statements are thoughts and which are emotions. Remember, this can be very challenging and will probably require some practice for you to get good at it.

Statement	Thought	Emotion
I'm worried about throwing up.		
My plane is going to crash.		
I'll never be able to go outside again.		
I'm frustrated that I cannot do this perfectly.		
A really big thunderstorm is coming.		
I'm so mad that my mom made me go to the doctor.		
When I eat greasy food, I get really sick.		
I know that dog is going to hurt me.		
I love spending time with my friends.		
Being in the dark scares me.		

The Spiraling STAIRS

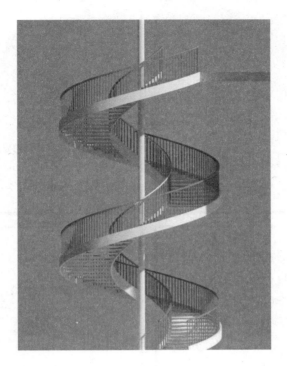

Now that you understand basic patterns, we're going to get a little more detailed. Check out another pattern: the spiraling stairs. There is even a fireman's pole through the middle to slide down. We're going to use this pattern to help you better understand your phobia.

Let's start with a typical phobia pattern. There are several parts involved that tend to repeat over and over. First, there is some type of situation that triggers (or starts) the pattern. Once in the situation, you have certain thoughts about what is going on, possibly without even realizing it; these thoughts are your automatic interpretation of what is happening. Next (or even at the same time), you'll have an emotional or physical reaction. Then, all these parts will lead to the safety behavior or action you take in order to be more comfortable. Check out the pattern below:

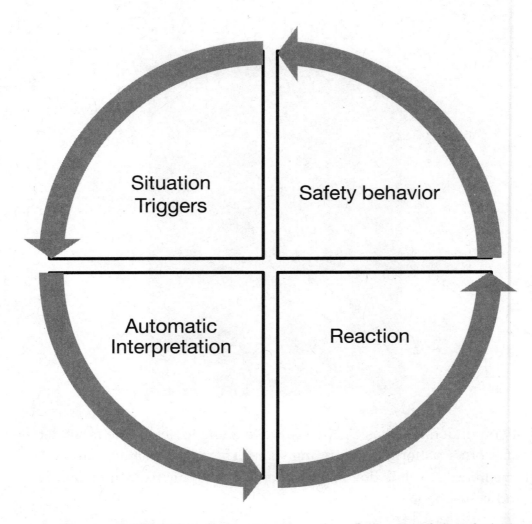

You can use the word STAIRS to help you remember the parts of the phobia pattern:

- **S**ituation

- **T**riggers

- **A**utomatic

- **I**nterpretations

- **R**eactions

- **S**afety behaviors

Now, let's look a little closer at each step.

Situation Triggers

The situation that starts the phobia pattern can be of any type, at any time. However, the types of situations that trigger one person may not necessarily trigger someone else. For example, Courtney and Jack both have a fear of being alone. Courtney's phobia is usually triggered when her parents leave the room, while Jack's is triggered when no one is around him.

The situation that starts the pattern could also be a thought or physical sensation without any change in the environment. For instance, Aiden is watching his favorite TV show, and a thought pops into his head about a possible thunderstorm tomorrow. Mackenzie is lying down in bed, and her heart starts beating fast. Both of these experiences can trigger the pattern.

Automatic Interpretations

Our brains are constantly taking in information and interpreting it. Basically, we're trying to figure out the meaning of things. In many situations, our thinking tends to be so automatic that we may not even realize what thoughts are influencing us.

Have you ever had a totally different opinion about a situation than someone else? People can have similar experiences and very different interpretations of that experience. For instance, Hannah and Matthew are the same age and going to the same party. When they walk into the party, they see lots of people and hear loud music. Matthew views this party as fun! He likes the music, sees some friends across the room, and thinks people will be happy to see him. Hannah, on the other hand, thinks the music is too loud and that no one at the party will want to talk to her. Even though they are in the same situation, they have very different thoughts about what is happening.

So why do they have such different interpretations? A lot of it has to do with previous experiences and learning. Matthew had a lot of positive experiences at social events when he was growing up and therefore feels confident in his socializing skills. He also has an older brother who constantly plays loud music in their room, so he's used to it. Hannah is shyer and hasn't gone to many social events, so she hasn't had much practice in these types of situations. She's also an only child in a quiet household. You can see how their past experiences and learning might have led to very different interpretations of this situation.

Also, certain ways of thinking are more likely to continue the phobia pattern than others. For example, negative thoughts about ourselves, others, and the world are likely to fuel a phobia. Such thoughts might include:

- I can't handle this.

- I'm stupid.

- They think I'm boring.

- Other people will judge me.

- The world is dangerous.

- What if something bad happens?

Most of the time, these beliefs are highly exaggerated or not true at all, which means our interpretations can be wrong. Think back to chapter 1, when you learned about false alarms. False alarms are just another misinterpretation of a situation.

Reactions

Once we make interpretations, we automatically react. These reactions can take the form of physical sensations or emotions. Physical sensations are bodily reactions, such as increased heart rate, shakiness, or sweating. Emotions are the way you feel or your personal experience, such as love, happiness, fear, sadness, and anger.

Scientists argue about whether thoughts cause emotions, emotions cause thoughts, or they happen at the same time. For the purpose of understanding your phobia, just know that they work very closely together. Think back to Matthew and Hannah at the party. While Matthew's interpretation led to excitement and happiness, Hannah's led to nervousness and discomfort. Many people use the words "spinning," "tornado," or "roller coaster" to explain the mix of thoughts, emotions, and physical sensations they feel when they are faced with their phobic situation.

Safety Behaviors

A safety behavior is an action we take in order to provide relief or reduce discomfort. Think about what it feels like to be in the spinning tornado of thoughts and emotions. What do you usually want to do? Most people want to escape as soon as possible. This is not surprising. It's a natural instinct for us to want to protect ourselves and become more comfortable. In some cases, people even avoid situations so there is less of a chance they'll have to feel uncomfortable. Basically, people use safety behaviors to reduce negative feelings in the moment. In some situations, other people might even help us use these behaviors. Here are some examples:

- Instead of using the elevator or escalator, Owen takes the stairs. He is afraid that the elevator and escalator will both break down.

- Megan requires an adult to hold her hand at all times in stores so she does not get lost.

- Abigail will eat only organic, low-fat foods she has prepared herself to make sure she doesn't gain weight or get sick.

- Caitlyn only drives during the day and in good weather to reduce the likelihood of an accident.

- Carter refuses to go outside in the summer because he might be stung by a bee.

Although safety behaviors seem helpful in the moment, they actually maintain phobias. There are several reasons for this. First, a safety behavior supports the idea that a threat is actually present or likely; otherwise, we wouldn't need the behavior at all. A safety behavior also sends the message that we can't handle the particular situation we're avoiding, or we can handle it only if we do the behavior. In addition, a safety behavior reduces discomfort for only a short period of time. It does not actually make the phobia go away. So the next time a similar situation presents itself, the pattern will repeat itself. This is how phobias stick around.

Safety behaviors are tricky because in the moment they don't seem like a big deal. For example, does it actually matter if you like to drive during the day? Or that you take the stairs? Not really. But you have to ask yourself how important the behavior really is. What would happen without it? Would you have a really hard time, or fall apart? If so, we know there is a problem.

Now let's put it all together, using the parts of the phobia pattern (STAIRS) and our image of the spiraling stairs. Picture yourself at the bottom of the stairs when you come across a situation that may trigger your phobia. You start climbing the spiraling stairs, going in circles, higher and higher. This spiraling is the mix of automatic interpretations and reactions that can make you spin and feel that uncomfortable feeling. You finally reach the top of the stairs, your breaking point, where you don't think you can handle it anymore. So you slide down the fireman's pole for safety and relief. You use a safety behavior to escape and you feel better. However, this same pattern will repeat over and over each time you come across another similar situation.

Identifying the Spiraling STAIRS in Others

Sometimes it's easier to look at others' patterns first. Then you can make sure you understand the phobia pattern before working on your own. These can be tricky, so try not to feel discouraged if you don't get it right away. Do your best to see if you can identify what maintains Nicole and Logan's phobias:

Nicole and her family like to volunteer in the community. They recently heard about a group going to Ecuador to help with sea turtle conservation. Nicole loves animals and thought she would really enjoy this trip. However, she doesn't like flying. She hasn't been on a plane in six years, forcing her parents to drive for all their vacations. Nicole's fear started after hearing about a plane crash on the news. TV stations continued to show pictures of the crash and reported that the accident was due to a mechanical failure. Even though Nicole previously enjoyed flying, she now believes that planes are unsafe and that she will die if she flies again. Her parents tried to get her to fly a few years ago, and it was a total disaster. They went to the airport and waited at the gate. Nicole was fine until she saw the plane they would be on. She watched the workers fuel up the plane and load the luggage. When she didn't see anyone inspecting the plane, she began to worry. Nicole believed that the workers and pilot forgot to check the plane and wouldn't know if something were broken. She started to feel panicked. She felt really hot and sweaty, was breathing really fast, and started to get dizzy. She could not calm herself down and she began to cry. Nicole begged her parents not to fly because she thought they would all die. So they went home and drove the next day instead.

Take some of the information from Nicole's story and write it in the correct section of her phobia pattern:

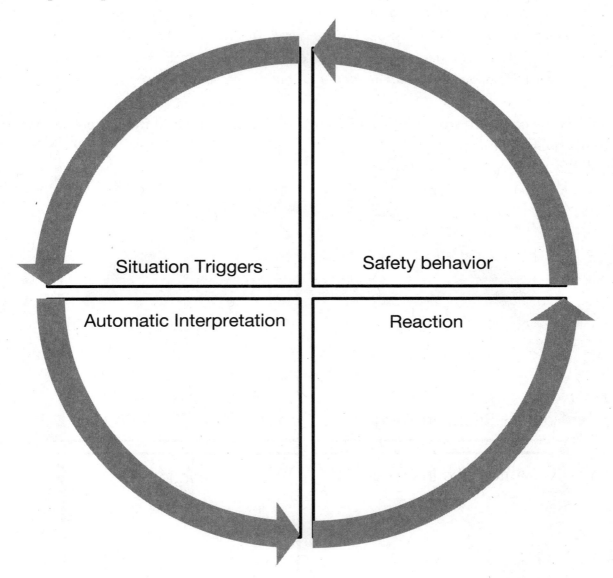

Let's look at another example:

Logan loves to play sports and is on his school soccer team. A few weeks ago, during one of his games, his mother had the coach pull him off the field, with the news that his dad had a heart attack at work and was in an ambulance going to the hospital. Logan was terrified that his dad might not make it. He cried on the way to the hospital, while also trying to be strong for his mom. At the hospital, he felt very antsy and on edge. After waiting hours in the waiting room, Logan finally heard that his dad would be okay. He was immediately relieved. Three days later, Logan had another soccer game, but something really odd happened. When he began to run, he panicked. Logan knew heart disease was genetic, so he was afraid that if his heart started beating too fast he would have a heart attack just like his dad. He started shaking and breathing really heavily. Logan raised his hand and got out of the game as soon as possible. He told his coach what had happened, and he sat out for the rest of the game.

Take some of the information from Logan's story and write it in the correct section of his phobia pattern:

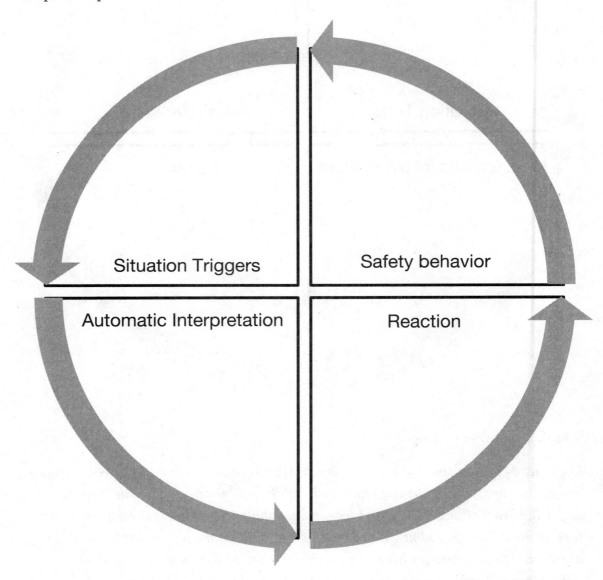

Identifying Your Spiraling STAIRS

Now it's your turn. This step is one of the most important parts of conquering your phobia. In order to figure out ways to help yourself, you need to understand your phobia pattern inside and out. Like any good scientist, you need some data first. You'll want to collect several samples or examples in order to see your full pattern. This process also helps you increase your awareness about each part of your phobia, since you are looking at it more closely or from a different perspective than you have before.

Use the following chart to collect data over the next few days or even weeks. You can also use past examples if you remember them. There is a column for each part of your phobia pattern.

Date	Situation Triggers	Automatic Interpretations	Reactions	Safety Behaviors

After you collect your data, come back to this page to fill in your complete phobia pattern based on your observations. If you have several phobias, you might have several different patterns.

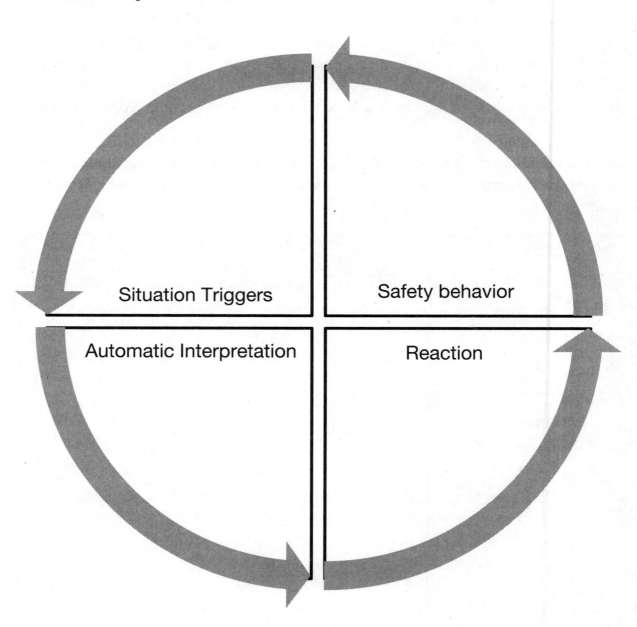

Congratulations! You accomplished a very important life skill: observing your own behavior in order to learn from it. Ideally, this awareness has helped you recognize what may have led your phobia to stick around for as long as it has. And although your pattern makes sense because it helps you feel better in the moment, hopefully you can see how it is only a short-term fix and not a long-term solution. The next chapter will focus on how you can alter your patterns to create a more long-term solution and ultimately conquer your phobia.

Chapter 4

How to FACE Your Phobia

If you run into a wall, don't turn around and give up.
Figure out how to climb it, go through it, or work around it.

—Michael Jordan, NBA champion and Most Valuable Player

Now that you understand more about yourself and your phobia patterns, it's time to figure out what you can actually do about it. In this chapter, you'll reflect on the times you've tried to make changes in the past and think about what may have gone wrong. This is critical information to help with future changes. You'll also learn about FACE strategies, a set of skills you can use to successfully break up your phobia patterns. So let's start making a plan to conquer your phobia!

What Didn't Work

Making changes that truly affect our lives on a daily basis is often quite difficult. It's common that our first few attempts are hard to stick to or don't work out so well. This is called trial and error. We try something and see if it works. If it doesn't, we problem solve and try again. Let's think about what hasn't worked for you so far.

What attempts have you made to conquer your phobia that didn't seem to work?

_____

_____

_____

Why do you think they didn't work? _____

_____

_____

_____

Why was change hard? _____

_____

_____

_____

Let's talk about obstacles people typically come across when they try to conquer their phobias. As you read, put a check mark next to the ones you've encountered.

☐ **Not knowing where to start**

Many people get overwhelmed by the amount of advice and information in the world, and they just don't know where to start. Others attempt to put some strategies into action but fall short because they don't have a specific plan. For example, a general plan like "I'm going to face my fear of bugs" won't work as well as a detailed plan: "For five minutes, I'm going to lie in the grass where there might be bugs."

☐ **Immediate comfort**

No one likes to feel uncomfortable, and many people do whatever they can to decrease their discomfort as soon as possible, such as escaping from certain situations. This is a short-term solution that makes you feel better in the moment. However, when you focus on short-term comfort, more important long-term goals, like learning to tolerate discomfort and facing the fear, are never realized. In the end, instant relief and constant comfort keep your phobia pattern spinning.

53

☐ **Difficulty with change**

Change is hard for everyone, whether you're trying to alter something big or small. It can be especially hard for people who like routine and structure, because doing things differently or trying new things often feels weird. Deciding to change the way you've been doing something for a long time can also be scary. Some people decide they cannot change or they are afraid to because they don't know what will happen.

☐ **Not a priority**

People have different opinions about what is important at different times in their lives. Priorities shift because of age, time of year, or even stress level. The people in our lives can also have an influence on our priorities. But ultimately, for you to conquer your fear, change has to become a priority and stay a priority. People often begin the process of conquering their fear, but then other things in their lives seem more important, become the focus, and take all their time.

☐ **Low effort and motivation**

It's also difficult to keep up our energy and motivation when we're working on a challenging task. How many people do you know who start things and never finish them? Sometimes this is because we think change should be easy and we find out along the way that it isn't. Other times, we tell ourselves it's not worth the effort or our efforts will never pay off. Whatever the reason, our energy decreases and we stop moving toward our goals.

☐ **The wrong kind of support**

Sometimes it's hard to find encouraging people who understand and support the changes you're trying to make. Even if you try really hard to make changes, you might continue to hear the wrong kind of messages from others. Friends or family might continue to support messages and behaviors that feed into your phobia rather than change it.

☐ **A lot of talk and no action**

Some people have done tons of research and know everything there is to know about fear and phobias. They know exactly what they need to do, but they never actually put it into action. This might be related to many of the reasons mentioned above. And some people are just afraid to fail. We can always come up with plenty of reasons not to do something.

☐ **Expecting results too soon**

Everyone wants change to happen quickly. People often try something for a few days and decide it doesn't work if they don't see immediate results. Many of us tend to give up too easily on things that might actually be helpful if we gave them the time they require to work. For example, will lifting weights for three days make you strong? Of course not! You have to keep exercising regularly to build up muscles. Change takes time.

☐ **No celebrations**

It's important to give yourself credit when you take a risk, overcome an obstacle, or try something new. However, we often focus on what we aren't doing rather than rewarding ourselves for the small steps we take toward change. If we don't celebrate our successes, we're missing out on opportunities to recognize growth and build confidence in our ability to change.

☐ **Stopping when things start to get better**

When people find success and notice improvements in their phobias, some are motivated to keep doing what is working. Others start to feel better and stop working at it, expecting their success to continue without effort. You can probably guess what happens next.

So many obstacles! No wonder it's hard to make changes happen, especially if you're not aware of what might get in your way.

Look back at your list of attempts. Now that you know about all the obstacles, why else do you think your earlier attempts didn't work?

_____

_____

_____

_____

It's okay to come up against obstacles. Don't get discouraged. Many people find success after multiple failed attempts. Sometimes we first have to figure out what doesn't work in order to get to what does. Here are some examples of famous people who had to overcome many obstacles before they made it work.

- Thomas Edison made over 1,000 attempts at the light bulb before he was successful, leading him to state that "the light bulb was an invention with a thousand steps."

- Dr. Seuss's first book was rejected by twenty-seven different publishers, and now he is one of the most famous children's authors.

- Walt Disney was fired by a newspaper due to lack of imagination and good ideas. He was also told Mickey Mouse would not work because the character would scare women. Now Disney is known all over the world.

- Colonel Sanders's secret chicken recipe, now known as Kentucky Fried Chicken's Original Recipe, was rejected more than a thousand times before a restaurant wanted it.

What Can Change?

Let's take care of some of these obstacles right now. The good news is that you are further along than most people because you have already explored your phobia patterns. By recognizing what keeps your phobia going, you can work on a specific plan to break up these patterns. You'll want to focus on small steps toward the long-term goal of conquering your phobia.

Using the typical phobia pattern below, let's think about what needs to change.

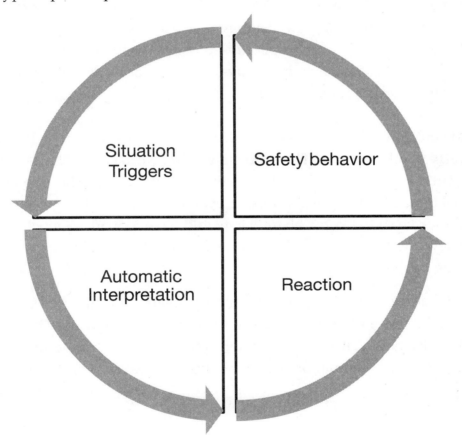

What areas do we have some control over, and where do we not have as much control?

_____

_____

_____

Situation Triggers

Let's start with the situations that trigger our phobias. Do we really have so much control over our environments that we could change every situation to make sure it doesn't trigger our phobias? Not really. We might like to think we do, especially since you've probably become very skilled at avoiding certain situations. However, the reality is that we cannot entirely control everything that happens around us.

Lucas doesn't like the feeling of insects or bugs touching his skin. He's also afraid he'll be bitten by rare insects and end up with an incurable disease. Lucas does everything he can to stay away from bugs. He stays inside as much as possible. If he has to go outside, he covers his exposed skin and runs as fast as he can to the car. He covers the cracks of the doors and windows in his house with tape. Before he goes to sleep, he also checks his bed for possible invaders.

So what do you think about Lucas's ability to control bugs? It sounds like he is doing a pretty good job, right? The problem is that he can't control everything. There are still many different ways he might encounter a bug. There could be bugs in his school building, or at restaurants, or even in his house if they squeezed through a crack he didn't know about. He would have to work so much harder (to an impossible level) to try to cover all the possible situations—and there still might be something he missed.

The truth is that we might feel like we can control our environments (and we can to some extent), but we're kidding ourselves if we think we can control everything all the time. Because of this, it's actually better to try *not* to control the situations that trigger our phobias. The situation itself isn't actually the problem; the fear is.

Have you focused a lot of your energy on trying to change or control the situations that trigger your phobia?

_____

As relates to your phobia, what do you try to control?

_____

_____

_____

Are you able to control everything all the time?

_____

What are you not actually able to control?

_____

_____

_____

Automatic Interpretations

Do we have control over all the thoughts that run through our brains? No. We really can't control our automatic interpretations, the things that pop into our brains. We all have odd, random thoughts at times. This is normal. Unfortunately, people sometimes get stuck when they believe they can control all their thoughts. If thoughts come into their brains that seem strange, they feel like something is wrong with them because they are not able to control these thoughts.

What we do have control over is how we interpret our thoughts; we get to decide what we're going to think about our thoughts and what we're going to do. When a thought occurs, we can take it as true or we can recognize it as false, silly, or odd. Just like you would if someone told you some gossip, you get to decide if you believe the thought or not.

Fear and phobias like to give us many messages, usually scary and unhelpful ones. It can be easy to get in the habit of believing what the phobia tells us instead of questioning it and looking for the truth. So one of the areas we'll want to focus on is the conversation you're having with your phobia. You'll have to figure out what your phobia is saying to you and how you might be able to interpret these messages differently. This means increasing the flexibility of your thinking, which is the focus of chapter 6.

What is it like for you when you get stuck in your thoughts?

_____

_____

_____

_____

If you didn't always listen to your thoughts, what would be different?

_____

_____

_____

_____

Reactions

Think back to all the things your body does when it responds to a real threat or false alarm. Do you have the power to stop these reactions and feelings?

Think about how much control you actually have over your body. Do you have to tell your heart to beat? Do you have to tell your sweat glands to produce sweat to cool down your body? No, your body does all this for you. You don't have to control it. So why do we think we can or should control our bodies when we're scared?

The answer is we can't and we don't have to. If you were giving a presentation in front of a hundred people and someone told you to calm down, slow down your heart rate, and stop sweating, would you be able to do it? Probably not. Would you have to do it to survive? No. Your body is doing what it "thinks" it needs to do, and that's normal.

Instead of working really hard to control our physical and emotional reactions, we can better spend our time understanding why our bodies react the way they do and accepting that our reactions and feelings are natural. We can also work on coping skills to help us tolerate these reactions when they feel uncomfortable. This will be the focus of chapter 7. The good news is, by accepting these reactions and changing other parts of our patterns, the reactions tend to lose their power.

Do you try to control your physical reactions and emotions? How?

_____

_____

_____

_____

Does it actually work?

_____

_____

_____

_____

Safety Behaviors

Out of all the areas, we have the most control over our behaviors. Whether you realize it or not, we choose every action we take. We choose whether to sit down and watch TV or do our work. We choose whether to eat donuts or salad. We also choose whether to use a safety behavior or face our fear head-on.

When you are stuck in your phobia pattern, you might not feel like you have a choice. This is how most people feel, and this is how the phobia wants you to feel. But you do have a choice. When we use a safety behavior, we're choosing immediate relief over conquering the phobia in the long run. This is a very difficult decision to make.

To help you move away from your safety behaviors, you'll learn about a different behavior, called exposure, in chapters 8 and 9. You'll take small steps toward facing your phobia rather than letting it control you. Exposures also help you practice thinking flexibly and accepting your feelings.

Describe a time when you chose comfort over facing your fear.

_____

_____

_____

_____

Looking back, what do you think about that decision?

_____

_____

_____

Making a Plan to FACE Your Phobia

Now it's time to put the plan together, focusing on key areas of change. The picture below shows which areas of change will break up different parts of the phobia pattern.

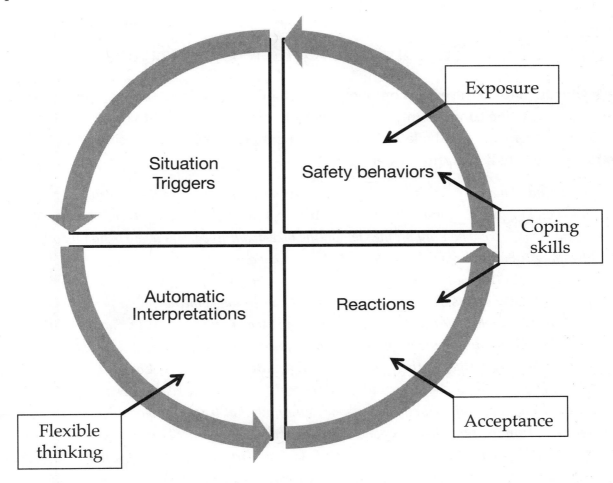

You can use the word FACE to help you remember the areas of change:

Flexible thinking

Acceptance

Coping skills

Exposure

As you continue reading this book, you'll notice that each of these important areas is addressed. There is a step-by-step path you can take to face your phobia. By embracing new strategies and altering your phobia pattern, you can conquer your phobia. Your brain and body will slowly make new associations and learn new phobia-free patterns.

Practice Breaking Phobia Patterns

It's your turn to be the expert on phobias. Pretend your friend Lily has come to you with a secret. She confides in you about her phobia and asks what you think she should do. As you read, look for Lily's phobia pattern to help you decide what FACE strategies might be helpful for her.

So, I kind of have a problem with blood. I'm not sure why or when it all started but it's been bugging me for about six years. At first, I just felt a little lightheaded when I saw blood. Like when my brother fell off his bike about five years ago. He had blood dripping from his forehead, and I had to turn away and sit down because I felt dizzy. I still feel guilty about not being able to help him, but I couldn't look at him. I never wanted to play sports or go to games because I was afraid someone might get hurt and there would be blood. At the time, I thought I just wasn't into sports, but now I think it was really because of the blood. I can't go to the doctor because I'm afraid someone will be bleeding in the waiting room or they'd want to give me a shot or take my blood. Even saying it creeps me out. And it seems to be getting worse. At first it was seeing blood that bothered me, but now it's anything that looks like blood. Red ink, red Jell-O, any red liquid—I'm gone. I get sweaty, and my heart beats really fast even just thinking about blood. It just makes me think of pain or something bad happening. So here's why I'm telling you this now: Last week I was with Elena watching a movie and her nose started bleeding. I freaked out. I ran upstairs, crying. I told her through the door she had to leave. I called her the next day to apologize, but I feel awful. And honestly, I'm afraid to be around her now because she might have another nosebleed. This stuff is totally out of hand. I feel like I can't do anything anymore because there might be blood. I don't know what to do.

Use the chart below to think about what might help Lily. First, fill in her phobia pattern. Then, using your knowledge about what you can and can't control, think about what advice you might give Lily. Also, look at the FACE strategies to help you decide which skills Lily might have to learn. This exercise is meant for you to brainstorm and challenge yourself. It does not have to be perfect. It will be a guide for you to use as you learn about each of the FACE strategies in later chapters.

Parts of the Phobia Pattern	Lily's Phobia Pattern	Possible FACE Strategies
Situation triggers		
Automatic interpretations		
Reactions		
Safety behaviors		

Great job! In understanding the FACE strategies, you have already started to overcome some of the obstacles that get in the way of success. As you keep reading this book, you'll also learn how to apply the FACE strategies yourself and create a path with specific steps to take toward long-term change. But first, we will address some of those other obstacles like motivation and priorities. It's time to get excited about change!

Chapter 5

Get Motivated to Make Changes

Courage is not the absence of fear, but the judgment that something
else is more important than fear.

—Edward Renaldi in *The Princess Diaries*

Before actually starting the process of change, it's good to think about why you
want to make a change. Since any change is challenging, you'll also need a little
inspiration to help you through the process. In this chapter, you'll consider whether
you are ready to make changes and how you can keep yourself motivated.

Are You Ready?

It's extremely normal for people to have mixed feelings about change. Most people
say there is a part of them that wants to change and a part of them that doesn't.
There is a part of them that wants to conquer their phobia and a part that thinks
it's better to just stay the same. This is called ambivalence, which basically means
having conflicting feelings about something.

People are also at different levels of readiness to make a change. Let's use Avery,
who has a fear of clowns, as an example.

- **Stage 1: No Change**

  Avery does not believe she has a problem. She thinks that it's normal to have
  a fear of clowns and that people who like clowns are crazy. She sees no reason
  to conquer her fear.

- **Stage 2: Considering Change**

  Avery is sitting at home while all her friends are at the fair. She is starting to see that her fear of clowns is getting in the way of having fun, but working on her fear seems like it will be really uncomfortable. Avery is thinking about the positive and negative aspects of change and has mixed feelings.

- **Stage 3: Preparing for Change**

  Now Avery is getting really frustrated. She's realizing all the things she doesn't do because of her phobia. She won't watch TV, go to the mall, or visit her grandma's nursing home because she's afraid a clown might appear. Avery has had enough and realizes it's time to do something about her phobia, even if that means working hard and being uncomfortable. She decides to talk to her parents about getting some help.

- **Stage 4: Actively Changing**

  Avery and her parents decide to read this book and meet with a psychologist to help her with her phobia. She starts to actively face her fear by thinking about clowns in a more flexible way (for example: *They are nice, friendly people in makeup* or *Movies use clowns to scare me on purpose*) and slowly taking steps to get closer to clowns. Her first step is to look at cartoon pictures of clowns. This makes her pretty tense, but she gets through it. She keeps challenging herself a little at a time.

- **Stage 5: Maintaining Change**

  Avery has been very successful in conquering her fear of clowns. She practices exposure by watching movies with clowns and going places where clowns might be. Last week she even hugged a clown. Avery feels much better around clowns now and no longer has to avoid so many different situations. She decides that she'll need to continue practicing her exposure to clowns regularly to make sure her phobia does not return.

What stage of change do you think you are in?

People move between these stages at different times in their lives. It's helpful to be honest about your stage of change. If you are having mixed feelings about change, it's important to address those concerns. Also, whether you have mixed feelings or are ready for action, you'll need to prepare yourself for the challenge by building up your motivation and support system.

Consider Your Values and Goals

To help you with possible mixed feelings and motivation, you should spend some time thinking about what is important to you. Values guide the direction you want to take in life, what you stand for, and the type of person you want to be. When you have a clear understanding of what you want out of life, you can work toward these values with your decisions and actions. Goals are specific tasks we try to complete. When these goals are in line with our values, we get closer and closer to leading the life we want to live.

Let's look at some examples:

Adam's Values and Goals

- Spending time with family and friends

- Getting into medical school

- Maintaining a healthy body through exercise and diet

- Traveling the world and having adventures

- Being up to date on technology

- Being honest with myself and others

Hailey's Values and Goals

- Having close relationships with my family

- Being a helpful and caring friend

- Volunteering in the community

- Working up to my potential in school

- Making a college basketball team

- Saving and using money wisely

Now it's your turn to write about your values and goals. These sentence starters can help you think about what to write:

- I value…

- I want to…

- It's important for me to…

- I would be fulfilled in life if I…

My Values and Goals

- _____

- _____

- _____

- _____

- _____

- _____

- _____

- _____

Your Phobia's Impact

Phobias are really good at getting in the way of what is important to us. Unfortunately, we don't usually take the time to notice how much our phobias are actually affecting our lives. To do this, you first have to consider your values, which you just did. Then, you have to think about how your phobia affects your ability to accomplish your goals and ultimately follow your values. Through this process, you can get a clearer picture of how your phobia is really influencing your life.

Let's look at Adam and Hailey again:

Adam's Phobia: Claustrophobia, or the fear of small, confined spaces	
Values and Goals	Impact
Family and social • Spending time with family and friends	• I miss out because I'm not willing to go to certain places to be with family, such as movie theaters, small restaurants, coffee shops, and some homes. • I will not ride in others' cars.
Academic and work • Getting into medical school	• I have difficulty with small classrooms, and I sometimes have to leave and miss information. • I'm nervous about wearing a mask on my face and being in small hospital rooms.
Health • Maintaining a healthy body through exercise and diet	• I only exercise outside, but I would like to be able to go to a gym to work out.
Interests • Traveling the world and having adventures • Being up to date on technology	• I have difficulty with public transportation, such as planes, trains, subways, and taxis. • I have to make sure hotel rooms are big enough. • No impact on technology.
Other values • Being honest with myself and others	• I tell myself my phobia is not a big deal, which is not true. • I sometimes hide my phobia, so I'm not being truly honest with others.

Hailey's Phobia: Illygnophobia, or fear of vertigo or dizziness (specifically from spinning and some heights)	
Values and Goals	Impact
Family • Having close relationships with my family	• I have difficulty playing with younger cousins on some playground equipment. • I miss out on some activities, like going to theme parks or skiing.
Social • Being a helpful and caring friend • Volunteering in the community	• No impact
Academic and work • Working up to my potential in school	• No impact
Interests • Making a college basketball team	• I avoid workouts that involve spinning.
Financial • Saving and using money wisely	• No impact

As you can see, the type and severity of the phobia might affect someone's life to varying degrees. While Adam's phobia seems to affect almost every area of his life in meaningful ways, Hailey's does not create as many problems.

Now that you've thought about what is important to you, think about how your phobia is affecting your quality of life. How does it get in the way of your values and goals? What are you missing out on? Write down the name of your phobia, or describe it. Then add your values and goals to the left column and the impact of your phobia to the right column.

My Phobia:	
Values and Goals	Impact
Family and social	
Academic and work	
Health	
Interests	
Financial	
Other values	

Looking at your chart, rate how much you think your phobia affects your life.

0	1	2	3	4	5	6	7	8	9	10

No impact   Some impact   High impact

You've identified what is important to you and recognized how your phobia is getting in the way. What do you think your future will look like if your phobia continues?

_____

_____

_____

_____

Benefits of Change

By thinking about the ways your phobia interferes with your life now and how it might continue to affect your life in the future, you might start to think of some reasons why you would want to conquer this phobia. Let's see how Adam is viewing his situation.

My phobia is constantly holding me back. I want to be free. I miss out on so much because my phobia restricts where I can go and what I can do. If I were able to conquer my phobia, I would be more social, have closer relationships, and feel more confident about my future career. I could go anywhere without having to worry about exits, crowds, or the size of the space. I would also have a lot more time to do the things I really want to do. I would be able to travel and visit all the places my phobia has kept me from going. Then I could honestly say I go on adventures rather than just wanting to. Without my phobia, I would come closer to being the person I want to be. I would have more opportunities in my future and feel more fulfilled in many areas of my life. I would feel like I am following my values rather than being held back.

And Hailey:

It would be nice to not have to miss out on some things that look fun. Without my phobia, it would be much easier to jump right in and be in the moment, rather than worrying about what my body might feel like. But honestly, my phobia does not keep me from following my values. I find other ways to get what I need, and I don't let my phobia keep me isolated. If my friends are doing something I have a hard time with, I still go along and socialize. I just don't do the activity. And these types of situations don't come up very often. Even with my phobia, I can be the person I want to be. If there is something I can do to make it better, I might, but I don't think my future will suffer too much if my phobia continues.

Adam and Hailey have very different experiences with their phobias. Adam has a lot of reasons why he would like to conquer his phobia, while Hailey is able to follow her values even with her phobia. It's probably not surprising that the more people's phobias affect their lives, the more they might benefit from change. This is because each individual has to weigh the costs versus the benefits of change and decide whether change is something that is important.

Take another look at your chart of values, goals, and impacts. Then, close your eyes for about five minutes and just think about how your life would be different without your phobia.

After you've visualized life without your phobia, look at these questions and write, in the space provided on the following page, about the benefits of conquering your phobia.

- Why do you want to be free from your phobia?

- What would you be able to do that you can't do now?

- What would you not have to do anymore?

- Would you be able to follow your values?

- Would you be the person you want to be?

- What does your future look like without your phobia?

_____

_____

_____

_____

_____

_____

_____

_____

_____

_____

How important is it for you to make this change?

0	1	2	3	4	5	6	7	8	9	10

Not important   Somewhat important   Very important

Building Your Motivation

Motivation is like a fuel source that energizes us or drives us toward action:

- Hunger drives us to eat.

- The desire to be healthy drives us to exercise.

- The desire to get good grades drives us to study.

- Wanting to win drives us to push harder in practice.

As you can see, there are many different types of motivation. Even in the same situation, people can be motivated in different ways. For instance, you might be motivated to organize your room because you don't want to get into trouble, while your friend might be motivated by the feeling of calm that a clean room provides.

Check what usually motivates you, keeping in mind that you might have different motivators in different situations. Add any others you think of.

- [ ] Money
- [ ] Fame or recognition
- [ ] Power or control
- [ ] Appearance to others
- [ ] Knowledge
- [ ] Growth or self-improvement
- [ ] Achievement or accomplishment
- [ ] Comfort or security
- [ ] Rewards
- [ ] Values or goals
- [ ] Connection or acceptance
- [ ] Need to contribute
- [ ] Morality
- [ ] Consequences or punishment
- [ ] Fear or distress
- [ ] Desire to prove someone wrong or to be right

☐ Major life events or changes (moving, divorce of parents, death of loved one)

☐ _____

☐ _____

Next, think about which motivational strategies might also help with your phobia. Adam realized he has a lot of motivation when it comes to exercising. He wakes up early in the morning to run, even when he's tired. He also seeks out opportunities to play sports with other people or do physical activities that are fun. He figured out that what works for him is having a specific goal (exercising five times a week), tracking his progress on his phone, and giving himself a reward when he reaches his goal. Adam also realized he is highly motivated by competitiveness in sports, so finding others who also like to exercise is helpful to him. With his interest in medicine, he also believes he should follow his values and practice what he'll be preaching to others about living a healthy lifestyle. Adam can take advantage of goal setting, tracking tools, rewards, competition, and values for motivation to work on his phobia as well.

What specific motivational strategies have been successful for you in the past?

_____

_____

_____

_____

What motivational strategies might also help you conquer your phobia?

_____

_____

_____

_____

People find additional inspiration in many different places. Some people are motivated by movies, speakers, books, art, photography, quotes, music, or others' stories. Support from others, like family, friends, teachers, or even psychologists, can also provide motivation.

Where might you find more inspiration and support?

_____

_____

_____

_____

Can You Change?

So is change actually possible? To help you decide, let's consider a few questions.

Do you know people who have made significant changes in their lives? If so, what did they change or overcome? If no one comes to mind, ask others this question.

_____

_____

_____

_____

What changes have you made in your life, big or small?

_____

_____

_____

_____

Let's go back to the original question: Is change possible?   Yes   No

People usually underestimate the likelihood that they will change in the future. Researchers surveyed 19,000 adults and found that they didn't believe they would change much in the future. However, they did recognize that they had changed a lot in the past. The study showed that growth continues throughout our whole lives, but we have a hard time believing it will happen.

In order to make change happen, you have to believe it can happen. And you have to believe you are capable of change just like anyone else. How confident are you that you can change?

0	1	2	3	4	5	6	7	8	9	10
Not confident				Somewhat confident					Very confident	

Not only do you need to believe change is possible, but you also have to be willing to change. Willingness means having an open mind about changes and taking some risks. It means doing things differently and seeing what other possible outcomes there may be. Willingness is about learning and being curious. When we face our phobias, we have to be willing to break our previous patterns to create a new experience.

How willing are you to change?

0	1	2	3	4	5	6	7	8	9	10
Not willing				Somewhat willing					Very willing	

Even better, let's go beyond "willing" and get excited! Think of coaches' pep talks in locker rooms before big games. The players and fans get so pumped up. Think about the motivational speeches given by great leaders, with thousands of people cheering in support. Shouldn't we be this excited about something that could change the rest of our lives?

If these inspirational leaders were getting ready to face a phobia, what would they say? How would they get excited and ready to take on a big challenge? Use their encouraging words to create your own personal pep talk.

_____

_____

_____

_____

_____

Committing to Change

Considering your values and goals, the impact of your phobia on your life, the benefits of change, and your levels of confidence and willingness, you have to decide if you are committed to conquering your phobia. This means taking responsibility for your own personal change, working hard to meet your goals, and not giving up.

How committed are you to conquering your phobia?

0	1	2	3	4	5	6	7	8	9	10
Not committed				Somewhat committed					Very committed	

If you answered the questions about importance, confidence, willingness, or commitment in this chapter with a 6 or lower, you might need to spend some more time thinking about your motivation to change before you take the next step. You may want to consider some of the following questions.

- What would need to happen to make conquering your phobia important?

- Do the costs of changing outweigh the benefits?

- What would make you more willing or confident?

- Is this the best time for you to make changes?

- What other support might you need?

If you are committed, create your own personal commitment statement.

The following example is Adam's statement:

I am willing and ready to take on the task of conquering my phobia. Even though this will be a challenge, I am willing to experience some discomfort now in order to meet my goal. I recognize that no one else can change this for me and that I will have to put in the time and energy to make it better. No excuses or obstacles will keep me from working toward my goal. I will ask others for support when I need it and be honest with myself about what is important.

My Personal Commitment to Change

_____

_____

_____

_____

_____

_____

_____

_____

_____ _____

Signature   Date

Once you have written your commitment statement, share it with the supportive people in your life. Explain your values and goals as well as the reasons change is important to you. It might also be helpful to have your list of values and goals, motivational pep talk, and commitment to change easily accessible. You could write these items on notecards or put them in your phone so you can find them easily whenever you need them.

Give yourself credit for the work you've done so far. You've figured out your phobia patterns, explored your feelings about change, and built up your motivation and support system. With all this great learning and self-exploration, it's time to put the plan into action. The next few chapters will teach you how to use the FACE strategies we've been discussing to conquer your phobia. Keep your mind open and your motivation strong!

Chapter 6

Have a New Conversation with Your Thoughts

You have to believe that something different can happen.

—Will Smith, actor, producer, and singer

It's time to learn more about the first FACE strategy to help you conquer your phobia. In chapter 3, you identified the automatic interpretations that were part of your phobia pattern. This chapter will focus on understanding these fear-based thoughts and moving toward more flexible thinking. By changing your thinking, you'll shift a crucial piece of your phobia pattern, which will shake things up and affect the rest of your pattern.

What Are Thoughts?

We're constantly thinking, and while we're aware of some of our thoughts, at times they're so automatic we don't even realize how they influence us. Thoughts are like luggage moving around an airport conveyor belt. Sometimes a thought enters your mind and leaves quickly (the bag that is taken off the conveyor belt); other times a thought just goes around and around (the bag that is left circling, unclaimed). Our brains are very active, and it's extremely difficult to just turn off our thoughts.

But what exactly are thoughts? Thoughts are ideas or opinions occurring suddenly in the mind. Notice that the words "idea" and "opinion" were used in the last sentence, not the word "fact." Many people mistakenly believe all their thoughts are true. The reality is that thoughts are just thoughts. Sometimes the things we think are accurate, and sometimes they are random or false. Let's test it out. Read these statements to yourself:

- I am a panda.

- It's 1962.

- I am going to win the lottery tomorrow (even though I didn't buy a ticket).

Now say them out loud. Whether you think them in your head or even say them out loud, these statements are not true. So it's clear just thinking something doesn't make it true or make it happen. We all have thoughts in our brains that are not accurate. We have to remember that thoughts are opinions or hypotheses that need to be further investigated. We have to take the time to determine whether they're true or false, as well as helpful or unhelpful.

Phobic Thoughts

Phobias take advantage of our thoughts. You learned in chapter 1 about the amygdala and how our fear keeps us safe in real threat situations. But when our phobias are in charge, we see things through a different lens. It's like we're using foggy binoculars. Instead of seeing the big picture, we're zooming in to look for possible danger. And to make matters worse, phobias make our lenses cloudy, and our views of situations get distorted. Our thoughts become inaccurate, negative, or unhelpful. We believe we're seeing things clearly even when we're not, which results in false alarms. Our phobic thoughts alert the amygdala when it's not necessary.

To separate yourself from your phobia, it can be helpful to picture it as something outside of yourself. Here are some images that can help you see the phobia as not actually part of you, but something you are struggling with:

- A bossy, older sister telling me what to do

- A big, mean bully picking on me

- An invader, like a little Martian, trying to control my brain

- Mud or quicksand that gets me stuck

- A bug buzzing in my ear

- A brick wall standing in my way

- An overly anxious bird sitting on my shoulder

What image or metaphor can you use for your phobia? Describe it with words and pictures here.

_____

_____

_____

Now that you have a way to picture your phobia, think about the messages it is usually sending you. It might be hard to remember your thoughts outside of an actual situation, but try to think back to times when you were scared. What was going through your head? You can also go back to the end of chapter 3 and look at your automatic interpretations as well.

What does your phobia usually say to you?

_____

_____

_____

_____

_____

Phobic Thought Traps

Everyone has worries, fears, and phobic thoughts at times. However, when this type of thinking is excessive or happens a lot, it might be a signal that you are in a phobic thought trap. When phobias take over our thinking, we tend to repeat the same negative, unhelpful, or false thoughts over and over. You are definitely not the only person who gets stuck, as there are several common thinking traps. See if you can remember times when you have been stuck in one of these traps.

Predicting the Negative

Our phobias want us to believe that something bad is very likely to happen. When we think about current or future situations, we assume the outcome will be negative. We're also very certain of this, even though we might not have lot of evidence to back it up. People report that they often rely on a feeling that something is going to go wrong. For example:

- I will get stuck in the elevator.

- The dog will bite me.

- I'm going to fail the test.

When have you predicted the negative?

_____

_____

_____

Generalizing

When something negative actually happens, our phobias can lead us to believe it will continue to happen in future situations. In other words, we're taking one experience and assuming the same outcome for all future cases. We might use words like "always," "every," "forever," or "never" to describe future experiences. For example:

- (*After choking*) I will choke on any piece of food that is not chewed fifteen times.

- (*After hearing news about a bridge falling*) Every bridge is unsafe and will collapse.

- (*After being chased by a bird*) Birds are never friendly and will always hurt me.

When have you generalized from one negative incident to future situations?

_____

_____

_____

Exaggerating the Severity

When we use exaggeration, we believe the situation will be horrible, dangerous, or intolerable. Our phobias can make us think about the very worst thing that could possibly happen. Thinking this way is called *catastrophizing*, or blowing things out of proportion. We're viewing the situation as worse than it actually is. One way to catch this type of thinking is to look for extreme language such as "terrible" or "disaster." For example:

- If I throw up, it will be a total disaster.

- If I make a mistake, I will never be successful in my life.

- There is going to be a terrible storm this weekend, and I don't think we can survive it.

When have you exaggerated the severity of a situation?

_____

_____

_____

Demanding Certainty

Many people with phobias feel like they need to be 100 percent sure that everything is going to be okay before they're willing to move forward. This need for certainty results in a need for control over most situations. We think that if we have control, nothing bad can happen. Some examples of this type of thinking:

- I need to know exactly what is going to happen in order to be okay.

- I must prepare for all possibilities.

- I would rather be safe than sorry.

When have you demanded certainty before doing something?

_____

_____

_____

Underestimating Abilities

Phobias also want us to believe we're weak and vulnerable, and there is nothing we can do about it. We tend to think we can't handle difficult situations, or there is no way we can get through them. We completely forget about our abilities and become defeated. For example:

- I will fall apart.

- I can't handle this, so I have to escape.

- This is too much for me.

When have you underestimated your abilities?

_____

_____

_____

You probably noticed a bit of a theme. When we're stuck in these phobic traps, we tend to make assumptions, jump to conclusions, and predict the future. But, in almost all the phobic situations we find ourselves in, nothing bad has actually happened. We're just really worried something bad *might* happen. Phobias take advantage of our imaginations and our ability to guess what could be coming next. They let us focus only on the negative side of things, which ultimately triggers a false alarm.

We all misinterpret things every now and then. But when we're stuck in the grips of a phobia, we tend to have trouble seeing things clearly. So it's important to learn how to catch yourself falling into the phobic thought traps. Now that you know about the different traps, let's see if you can pick them out of Camilla's story:

I was so excited about my family's trip to Washington. I love history and couldn't wait to see all the famous landmarks and museums. I spent hours and hours researching which places I wanted to visit and really hoped my family would be willing to follow along. The flight to DC was pretty cool, because I could see some of the monuments when we landed. But when we were leaving the airport, my sister told me we were taking the Metro to our hotel. I dropped my luggage and froze. I asked my parents if we could take a taxi instead, but they just rolled their eyes and told me it would be fine. It was not going to be fine! Last time I rode a subway, it got stuck underground. It was terrifying. It felt like we were stuck forever. No way was I doing that again! If I got on that train, I knew it would get stuck. Then we would be sitting underground with tons of people crowded in that tiny space. And what if no one could get to us for hours? I would freak out!

💬 Which phobic thought traps did Camilla fall into? Give examples of her thinking.

☐ Predicting the negative: _____

☐ Generalizing: _____

☐ Exaggerating the severity: _____

☐ Demanding certainty: _____

☐ Underestimating abilities: _____

Here's Victor's story:

I love sports and think I'm a pretty good athlete. Lately, I've been doing a lot of running and training for a marathon. Part of my training included some 5K races. Since I was doing these types of races, my friends asked me if I wanted to challenge myself and do some races that included mud and obstacles. I thought it would be pretty fun, so I said sure. On the day of the race, I was feeling pretty good. I knew my group would stay together and I just tried to enjoy the experience. Some obstacles were really easy, like jumping over walls or crawling through the mud. I was the fastest runner in our group, so I had to slow down every once in a while to let the others catch up. We were making good time and I felt really confident, until I saw one of the very last obstacles. There was a huge hole filled with muddy water, and a wall above it. You had to go completely underwater to get past the wall. I've never had any problems swimming, but for some reason the muddy water was just too much. I couldn't get past not knowing what was in there and not being able to see at all. I just kept thinking about what could be in the water. There was a part of me that knew I wouldn't die and the likelihood of something horrible happening was low, but it didn't matter. I couldn't make myself do it.

Which phobic thought traps did Victor fall into? Give examples of his thinking.

☐ Predicting the negative: _____

☐ Generalizing: _____

☐ Exaggerating the severity: _____

☐ Demanding certainty: _____

☐ Underestimating abilities: _____

Apply your new learning to your own phobic thoughts. Which phobic thought traps do you fall into? Give examples of your thinking.

Predicting the negative: _____

_____

Generalizing: _____

_____

Exaggerating the severity: _____

_____

Demanding certainty: _____

_____

Underestimating abilities: _____

_____

Choosing a Path

Our phobic thoughts seem to have a lot of power, especially when we automatically believe they are true. The STAIRS pattern showed how our automatic interpretations, or thoughts in the moment, have a big impact on our reactions and behaviors. It's the way we *think* about a situation that leads to how we feel and behave, not the situation itself. So rather than taking our thoughts as facts, we need to spend some time thinking about our thinking.

Some people believe they need to just stop thinking. They want to push away scary, phobic thoughts. This seems to makes sense, but it's exactly the opposite of what we want to do. It's very hard not to think. People have also found that the more they try not to think about something, the more they actually think about it. Trying to push away phobic thoughts or not have them at all is probably not going to work very well.

Instead, we can notice a phobic thought and decide what we want to do with it. When we have a phobic thought, there are two main paths we can take. It's our decision which one we choose.

Path 1: Let's call this the *haunted house* path. When we interpret situations, we tend to use phobic thinking.

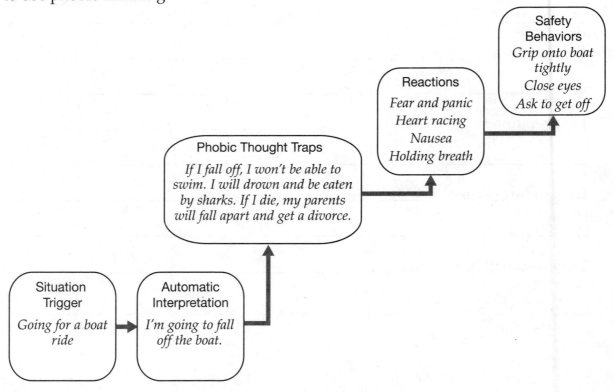

As you can see, continuing with phobic thinking doesn't end very well. It includes a lot of discomfort and ultimately results in us missing out on things. So what other option do we have?

Path 2: Let's call this the *scientific path*. This is the path we take when we use experiments. Instead of just believing all our thoughts, we're going to put them to the test. To do this, we need the smart part of our brain, which is called the prefrontal cortex, to be working hard. This part of the brain helps us with decision making, problem solving, reasoning, and logical thinking. Let's see what happens when we use it.

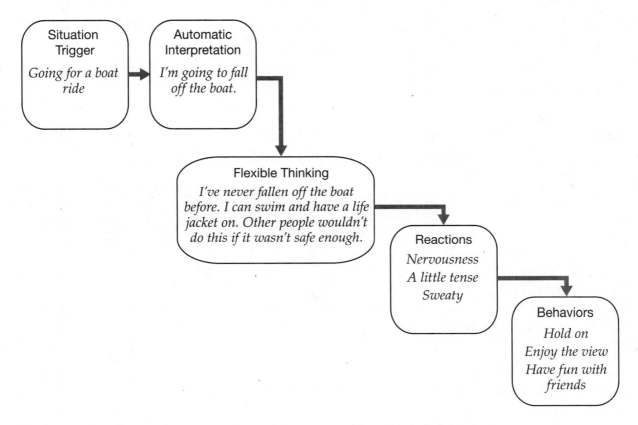

In this example, the situation and initial automatic interpretation are exactly the same as in the earlier one. However, instead of accepting the thought *I'm going to fall off the boat* as true, we put it to the test. By using our smart brains and not falling into the phobia's trap, we were able to come up with some very logical and realistic thoughts. This might not take all the discomfort away, but in the end going on the boat ride seems like a much more enjoyable experience. Also, if you get off the boat, you'll never know if any of the phobic thoughts are really true. By staying on the boat and testing it out, you get to see what actually happens.

Let's practice with another example:

Dominic has an interview tomorrow to work at a summer camp. He prepared for his interview all week. He's not entirely sure he's qualified for the job, but he thinks he can win them over with his personality. This morning, his friend, who also wants to work at the camp, called to tell Dominic about his own interview. He said the directors were very serious and asked really tough questions. Dominic starts to wonder if he should even bother, and he stays up worrying all night. The next morning, he wakes up with a really bad stomachache. He immediately thinks, I have an ulcer. *Dominic often worries about getting an ulcer. One of his teachers had to stop teaching in the middle of the school year because of her ulcer.*

Based on his initial thought, *I have an ulcer,* which thoughts will take Dominic down the phobic path and which thoughts will take him down the scientific path?

Thoughts	Path 1: Haunted House (Phobia)	Path 2: Scientific (Smart Brain)
The likelihood that this is an ulcer is probably low.		
I'll never be able to get this job, or any job.		
There is something wrong with me.		
My stomach might hurt because I'm nervous about the interview.		
I need to go to the doctor now.		
I'm going to die.		
I've had stomachaches before and it wasn't an ulcer.		
I ate really greasy food last night.		
I can get through this.		

The lesson here is to stop and think about your thinking. Even though we can't control every thought that enters our brains, we can decide how we're going to think about our thoughts. We know phobias give us scary and false messages, but we get to decide whether we're going to listen.

A worksheet depicting the two paths is available online for you to download. You can use this to help you practice moving from phobic thought traps to more flexible thinking.

Flexible Thinking

When you think of flexibility, perhaps you picture a rubber band or people who can bend themselves into pretzels. Things that are flexible are usually stretchy, adjustable, and bendy. Think about what a tree would be like if it were flexible. It would sway and bend with the wind. People also show flexibility by going with the flow and seeing things from different perspectives. When we think in flexible ways, we're more likely to be open-minded and willing to search for other possibilities.

Our phobic thought traps make it very difficult to be flexible. Phobic thoughts are rigid and limiting. When you think of rigidity, you might picture a concrete block or a hammer, because rigid objects are hard and unbending. Think about what a tree would be like if it were rigid. Its branches would snap and break in the wind. People with rigid thinking (you might also call them stubborn, stuck, or hardheaded) tend to have extreme thoughts that they are unwilling to change. It's also very hard for them to see things in a different way.

Our goal, then, is to move away from extreme, rigid, and phobic thoughts (path 1) toward more realistic, reasonable, and flexible thoughts (path 2). Even if your phobic thoughts have been around for a long time, it's possible for you to move to a different path. There are three main steps to help you become a more flexible thinker:

1. Recognize phobic thinking.

   If you aren't able to admit your thinking might be a little rigid, it will be very difficult to make any meaningful changes. Phobic thoughts and worries are going to pop up; it's normal for this to happen (and helpful when there is a real threat). We don't need to be surprised or shocked, especially if these thoughts have been around for a while; we can almost expect them to come knocking. Instead of trying to ignore them or being really afraid of them, try to accept that these thoughts are just thoughts.

2. Create some distance from your thoughts.

We create distance from our thoughts by hearing what our thoughts are saying, but not necessarily listening. Using an image or metaphor for your phobia, you can say something like:

- Oh, that mud is trying to get me stuck again.

- I know the brick wall is trying to protect me, but I can handle this.

- Hello, anxious bird. I hear you, but I think you are exaggerating.

By stepping back and not listening to everything your phobia tells you, it's easier to move toward flexibility. Sometimes your phobia may whisper to you and sometimes it might scream. Either way, you don't have to listen. You can keep going, do what you want to do, and follow your values. Show your phobic thoughts who's boss!

3. Challenge your phobic thoughts.

There are many different ways you can do this. Some people like to picture themselves arguing with their thoughts or challenging their thoughts to a duel. Others like to imagine their thoughts being put on trial in order to determine the truth. Another way is to picture each situation as a movie, where you need to go behind the scenes in order to see what is really happening. Whichever creative way you like to think about it, the goal is still the same. We want to work toward more realistic, flexible thinking.

Challenging Your Phobic Thoughts

Picture someone actually falling into a hole or a trap of some kind. This person has two options: to just lie there and surrender to the hole, or to do some problem solving and find a way out. When we listen to our phobic thoughts, it's like we're giving in and giving up. Instead, we want to actively challenge this type of thinking so we can be free. The less time we spend in phobic thought traps, the more time we have for the things we care about.

Since you've already identified your phobic thoughts, it's time to learn how to challenge them. There are many different ways to do this. What works for you might be different from what works for someone else. You have to find the strategies that fit best with your type of phobic thoughts. Remember, this is a process. You've probably spent quite a bit of time stuck in phobic thought traps, and it may take some time for you to shift your thinking. But you can do it! The more you practice, the easier it will get.

Rely on the Facts

Since our phobias want us to pay really close attention to those uncomfortable feelings or scary possibilities, we actually want to focus much more on facts. If we rely only on how we feel about a situation, we're missing a lot of really important information. We need to use that smart part of our brain and do some investigating.

Let's use Mason as an example. He has a fear of fire. If anything is burning, he thinks it will start a fire. He becomes extremely uncomfortable if he sees flames of any kind and demands the fire be put out immediately. Mason was asked to write down all the evidence he had to support his phobic thought and all the evidence against his phobic thought. He had to be reminded that evidence means facts, not feelings.

Mason's Phobic Thought: We can't light candles because it will start a fire and our house will burn down.	
Evidence For	Evidence Against
It has happened. There are stories on the news about people burning candles and their houses catching fire.	Fire is very common. People use it all the time for cooking, heating, and entertainment.
I just feel like something bad will happen. (Not a fact)	Not every flame turns into a destructive fire.
	We've burned candles before and nothing bad has happened.
	Even if the candle started a fire, it's not guaranteed the house would burn down.
	The news likes to report extreme cases, so this probably doesn't happen all the time.

See if relying on facts and evidence will help you with your phobic thoughts. If you are having a hard time coming up with facts, you might ask someone for suggestions.

My Phobic Thought:	
Evidence For	Evidence Against

Don't Predict—You're Not a Fortune-Teller

It would be really great if we could predict the future. Wouldn't that make things so much easier? Let's see how good you are at guessing what will happen.

Question	Your Prediction	What Actually Happened	Were You Right or Wrong?
How many texts will you get today?			
What is the first word you'll hear when you turn on the TV?			
How many bites of food will you have at dinner?			
What will the highest temperature be today?			
What will the final scores be for any games you watch today?			

How did you do? It was probably pretty difficult to make these kinds of predictions. However, our phobias want us to think we can. We start to believe we know (or feel) when something bad might happen, so we stay away from what we fear. But when we avoid something, we never really find out what actually would have happened because we don't stick around long enough. The truth is, we're not very good at predicting outcomes. We fool ourselves into thinking we're good at it because we tend to remember only the times we predicted the future correctly and forget the times we didn't.

Look at these negative predictions:

- I will get stuck in the elevator.

- The dog will bite me.

- I'm going to fail the test.

What do you think happens more often: that we predict a specific bad thing will happen and it does, or that we predict a specific bad thing will happen and it doesn't?

When you catch yourself making a negative prediction, stop and ask:

- Am I a fortune-teller?

- How accurate am I when I make predictions?

- When I've made specific predictions before, how often did they actually come true?

- Is it possible that something neutral or good could happen? What?

Crunch Some Numbers

When our phobias are telling us something bad is going to happen, often we're not being realistic about its probability, or the likelihood that it will actually happen. We get stuck on the idea that something could happen, even if it hasn't happened before.

Rather than depending on a feeling, it's better to trust real numbers. We can determine the likelihood of events occurring by examining how often the event has actually happened in the past. Now this is where it gets tricky. If we just look at the number of times something bad has happened, this number can be pretty scary. For example, if you heard on the news that seventy people in the United States died in recent earthquakes, you would probably start to worry more about earthquakes. Seventy! That seems like a lot, right? However, reporting rare or extreme incidents without actually giving us the full picture is a tactic frequently used by the media. In this particular case, they purposefully didn't mention that these seventy deaths took place in a nineteen-year period, from 1990 to 2009. Unfortunately, that means we're usually exposed to a lot of inaccurate information about the probability of danger.

Let's look at the numbers more closely. We can find the probability of an event by looking at how often the event has actually happened as well as how many opportunities there were for the event to happen. For example:

$$\text{Probability} = \frac{\text{Number of times the event has happened}}{\text{Number of times the event could have happened}} = \frac{70 \text{ deaths}}{60{,}807 \text{ earthquakes}}$$

Probability = 0.0011511%

So between 1990 and 2009, the chances of any earthquake resulting in death were less than one percent. Doesn't a chance of less than one percent sound a lot better than seventy deaths? When you look even more closely at the facts, you might find more details you didn't notice at first. In this case, sixty-seven of the seventy deaths took place in California. So if you live outside of California, the chances of encountering a fatal earthquake are even less.

Remember, those seventy deaths also occurred over nineteen years. They didn't happen all in one week or even in one year. But let's say they did all occur in 2010. The population of the United States in 2010 was 308,745,538 people. This would mean 1 out of every 4.4 million people died as the result of an earthquake that year. Definitely very unlikely!

Sometimes it might be hard to track down these types of numbers. Instead, you can ask yourself these questions:

- How likely is it that this will actually happen?

- What does my past experience tell me about the probability of this happening?

- Is it possible my views about this have been skewed by the media or rare circumstances?

- Do other people do or experience this without something bad happening to them?

You also have to look out for excuses you might have made in the past. People often come up with reasons for why things went well. For example, they might believe the only reason something bad didn't happen was because they were lucky. Or they prevented something bad from occurring that would have, if they had not intervened.

Laura believed as long as she had her purple socks on during her soccer games, she wouldn't get hurt. One day, she forgot her purple socks. She was really scared to play and tried to stay away from other players during the game. Once the game was over and she made it through without getting hurt, she decided she must have been okay because one of her teammates wore purple socks that day.

Laura's belief had nothing to do with the actual probability of her getting hurt. She was relying on superstitious thoughts rather than actual facts.

Ultimately, we have to be truthful with ourselves. The reality is that we all take risks every single day. Life would be pretty boring if we didn't. Think for a minute. What risks do you take on a regular basis that you hardly ever think about?

_____

_____

_____

_____

These risks are a part of life. We have to leave the house, get into a car, stand in buildings, eat food, breathe air, and much, much more. If we wanted to prevent all possible risk, we would literally have to live in bubbles—and even that would be risky. So in order to live full lives, we have to accept some amount of risk. We know there is always a chance something bad could happen, but the likelihood is pretty low. You might have to remind yourself that you take risks all the time. Your phobia just wants you to think you don't.

Be Realistic About the Past and Future

It's true that bad things happen sometimes. We get hurt, get scared, and make mistakes. This is completely normal. But our phobias take advantage of these negative situations by continually reminding us about what happened and maybe even exaggerating how bad it was. While it's helpful to think about past experiences for evidence, our phobias want us to remember only the negative experiences in our past in order to scare us. Basically, if something bad happened once, we start to think it's going to happen again and again.

To start challenging your phobic thoughts, you need to be very realistic about past events. Sometimes we don't remember things exactly as they were. Negative experiences in particular can become amplified as time goes on. And we usually focus more on the bad feeling we had than on the facts of the situation. So when you think about a past negative experience, try to focus on what was true.

- What actually happened in the past?

- Even though it felt bad, did I get through it?

- Is it possible it seems worse now than it actually was?

Also, remember that one isolated event does not make a pattern. Sometimes things happen once and that's it. We call it a fluke, an accident, or a rare circumstance. So instead of assuming something bad will happen in the future, think about how likely it is that the same situation will occur again. You can ask yourself:

- Am I generalizing from one past situation to all future situations?

- Is it possible the past situation was an exception?

- How likely is it that this will happen again and again?

Focus on the Present

Sometimes we worry that something really specific might happen. For example, after falling from a ladder, Theo believed he would fall every time he used a ladder. Other times, our phobias can be really general. Many people say they are afraid that something bad is going to happen. They don't even know what the bad thing might be; it's just going to be bad. This is very, very sneaky. Instead of being scared about just one thing, our phobias trick us into worrying about everything! If your phobia is being really general, try to dig a little deeper.

- What specific bad thing do I think is going to happen right now?

- If I can't think of something specific, is there really anything to worry about?

- Is my phobia tricking me into being overly cautious when I don't need to be?

Sometimes we get so wrapped up in what happened in the past and what might happen in the future that we forget to think about what is happening now. Practice focusing on the present moment.

- What is actually happening right now?

- Are there any real threats in the present moment, or is this a false alarm?

Deflate the Severity

When we use extreme words like "horrible" and "awful," it's like we're inflating or blowing up a balloon. The more we blow, the bigger it gets and the closer it is to popping. That is probably how you feel when things seem overwhelming and impossible: like you just might burst. In order to keep from bursting, we have to deflate the ballon, or let some air out of it.

You can start by choosing a few less extreme words and phrases. Add your own to the lists as well.

Extreme, Inflated Words/Phrases	Less Extreme, Deflated Words/Phrases
Awful	Challenging
Can't handle it	Difficult
Catastrophic	Disagreeable
Dangerous	Flexible
Disaster	Hurdle
End of the world	Interesting
Failure	Manageable
Going to die	Obstacle
Horrible	Perplexing
Impossible	Possible
Intolerable	Risky
Terrible	Troublesome
Unbearable	Uncomfortable
Worst	Unpleasant
_____	_____
_____	_____

By using deflated words, you're likely to get closer to the reality of the situation. When our emotions are high, especially fear, it might be hard to see the truth. For instance, think of a time when you were really scared, maybe a time years ago that has nothing to do with your phobia. Try to remember how you were feeling and the thoughts that went through your head at that moment. It would not be surprising if some inflated words popped up.

Previous scary situation: _____

My feelings and thoughts at the time: _____

_____

_____

Now come back to the present moment and think about what happened.

Was it horrifying or was it uncomfortable? _____

How long did the feeling last? (Forever?) _____

What was the outcome or consequences?_____

_____

Did I survive it? _____

Looking back, how might you see the situation differently now? What deflated words might be more appropriate for the situation?

_____

_____

_____

The concept of deflating the situation is extremely important to learn. We can tolerate uncomfortable feelings and manage difficult situations. And the truth is that we will all face some hard times in our lives, ones that can be unpleasant to experience. The good news is, it doesn't last forever and we can get through it! A happy life does not necessarily mean a life free from fear, sadness, or problems. A happy life is one where you can experience discomfort and continue on.

When you catch yourself exaggerating a situation, ask yourself:

- How can I deflate my balloon? What words are more realistic?

- Will this feeling last forever?

- What are the benefits of tolerating my discomfort?

- What is the most likely outcome?

- Can I survive this?

- How much will this matter a year from now?

Accept the Unknown

One of the reasons we do all this predicting and assuming is because we want to know what is going to happen next. We want to be prepared. We want to be in control so we can prevent bad things from happening. Seems pretty reasonable, right? But we're actually attempting to do something that has little chance of success. It's simply a waste of time.

It's hard to be 100 percent certain about anything. A lot of times when we think we're sure, we're just taking our best guess. For instance, are you 100 percent sure the TV will go on the next time you turn it on? How do you know for sure? Would you bet a million dollars on it? What if the cord was loose or unplugged? What if the circuits in the TV had burned out?

How sure are you? _____ percent

Let's try another one. Are you 100 percent sure the president of the United States is alive right now? How can you be sure? Is it possible something happened and you just don't know about it yet?

How sure are you? _____ percent

Our best guess is that the TV will turn on and the president is still living; however, we cannot be 100 percent, absolutely sure. And that's okay. We're sure enough. That is why you probably don't think about these kinds of things; most of the time you're sure enough not to spend any more time thinking about them. But sometimes, our phobias make us believe we have to be certain about something. At these times, instead of listening to your phobia, you can remind yourself that we're not really certain about anything, especially when it comes to predicting the future.

Am I wanting to be certain? About what? _____

_____

_____

Do I need to be 100 percent sure? Why or why not? _____

_____

_____

Have you ever heard the saying "anything is possible"? People usually use this saying to increase their motivation and willingness to explore. If anything is possible, we can set incredible goals and won't be held back by limitations. This phrase is also a reminder that it's normal to be uncertain. We don't know everything and we can't predict everything. By accepting the unknown, we accept some amount of risk, but we also allow for opportunity and growth.

Release Control

Along with believing we can be 100 percent certain, another myth we often believe is that we can be in complete control at all times. While you do have some control over the decisions you make and the actions you take, you don't have control over everything that happens to you. Even if you plan and think of all the possible things that could go wrong, you can never be 100 percent in control—especially since you have very little control over how *other* people act.

List some examples of things in your everyday life over which you have very little control.

_____

_____

_____

_____

What about your heartbeat, the weather, or what song comes on the radio? Can you control your friend's mood all the time? Do you get to decide whether someone is going to bump your car at a stoplight or not? Nope. We don't have control over these things and many, many others.

It's true that you can avoid certain situations. For example, you could decide to never ride in a car again so you don't get into an accident. However, as you learned in chapter 3, avoidance is a type of safety behavior that keeps phobias going. It doesn't fix the problem. You could also analyze every detail of a situation to predict every possible thing that could go wrong. But this kind of worry is very passive and unproductive. And thinking about all the possibilities doesn't actually keep anything bad from happening. Even with your greatest effort, it's not guaranteed that you can prevent a negative event.

Instead, we have to accept that we cannot prepare for everything. We cannot keep all bad things from happening. Our goal can instead be to live our lives bravely and see what happens.

Can you think of a time when you let go of control and just went with the flow? What happened?

_____

_____

_____

_____

Remember That You Are Capable

We often feel completely defeated by our phobias. Everything seems impossible and the words "I can't" become all too familiar. We want to escape to a fictional place where there are no problems. This self-doubt and belief that we're incapable leads to safety behaviors, which ultimately keep our phobia patterns going.

To conquer our phobias, we have to recognize our abilities, build our confidence, and be willing to face our fears. Instead of running from our fears, we want to become resilient. This means facing problems head-on, working through them, and then coming out on the other side. A resilient person is not someone who has no fears or problems, but someone who has learned to cope in difficult situations.

If our mind-set is that we'll face uncomfortable emotions and situations in our lives, but we're capable and can get through them, then all the what-ifs lose their power. We don't have to wonder if something bad will happen, because we're aware that eventually it will. And when it does, we can get through it. We don't have to be certain, because whatever the outcome is, we can handle it. We don't have to try to prepare or control, because we already have everything we need. Even in the worst of circumstances, we have the ability to cope. The more we let go and allow ourselves to work through discomfort, the more we will realize our strengths and abilities.

What were some difficult or uncomfortable situations in your life?

_____

_____

_____

_____

How did you get through them? _____

_____

_____

It's likely you've already had to overcome some pretty difficult challenges in your life. Unfortunately, we usually focus only on how tough something was, rather than on our strength and our ability to work through something difficult. Ultimately, problems and mistakes will come and go, and we can see these as opportunities to practice our coping skills and increase our resiliency. Rather than dwell on the problem, notice your growth and ability to handle problems.

When you feel vulnerable or defeated, consider these questions:

- Have I overcome something like this before?

- What steps can I take to move forward?

- What can I learn from this situation?

- Even though this is challenging, can I push through it?

Be Kind

It's also important to catch the critical voices that sometimes pop into our heads. While it's pretty easy for most people to be kind to others, for some reason, many of us are really hard on ourselves.

When you are afraid or have a problem, which critical statements do you say to yourself?

☐ I'm weak.		☐ This is too much for me.
☐ I can't handle this.		☐ I really messed up.
☐ I must be crazy.		☐ I can never do anything right.
☐ What is wrong with me?		☐ _____
☐ I'm such a loser.		☐ _____
☐ What did I do wrong?		☐ _____

Do you notice how critical and mean you can be to yourself? What would happen if you said these things to your friends? How would you feel if a friend said these things to you? You probably wouldn't have those friends for much longer, right? So why are we so hard on ourselves?

Some people think we need to be really critical in order to get ourselves motivated. But most of the time, this type of talk just makes us feel worse. We start to believe these things are true. So what can we do instead?

Think about what you would say to a friend who was afraid or having a problem. Then switch it around for yourself. Which statements might you use to replace the critical voice?

- This is really tough.

- I can get through this.

- Everyone struggles sometimes.

- I'm resilient.

- Everyone makes mistakes.

- I'm scared and that's okay.

- What went well?

- I can give it my best effort.

- I can take one step at a time.

- I've made it through tough times before.

- I'm stronger than I think.

- _____

- _____

- _____

Doesn't this sound so much better? And much more comforting? It's even more motivating. But it's not easy. As silly as it seems, we have to remind ourselves to be kind to ourselves.

Recognize Your Strengths

Since everyone is unique, we each have a different set of skills and abilities. It would be pretty boring if we were all the same. The trouble is, we usually spend more time focusing on what we're not good at, and ignore our strengths.

Spend a little time thinking about what you are good at and what characteristics you have that you would consider strengths. It can be anything from a particular academic or physical skill to a personality trait. It might seem hard at first, but try to list fifteen or more strengths. If you're having trouble, ask your friends and family about your strengths. You can even search online for lists of strengths and see which ones apply to you.

My List of Strengths

1. _____
2. _____
3. _____
4. _____
5. _____
6. _____
7. _____
8. _____
9. _____
10. _____
11. _____
12. _____
13. _____
14. _____
15. _____

Discover Courage

Think of courageous individuals in history or characters in the movies. What makes them courageous? Is it their fortune, their fame, or their good looks? Is it their ability to lead easy, comfortable lives? Probably not. Courage is defined as the ability and determination to face fear, danger, or difficulty. Here are a few examples of exceptionally courageous individuals in history:

- Helen Keller faced both deafness and blindness. She became a highly influential author, lecturer, and human rights activist.

- Orville and Wilbur Wright went through numerous obstacles and failures in order to create the first powered and piloted airplane. They crashed many times.

- Rosa Parks refused to give up her seat on a public bus just because of her skin color. Her action led to one of the largest movements against racial segregation in history.

Who is your model of courage? Why do you look up to that person?

_____

_____

_____

_____

When facing an obstacle, we have to talk ourselves through it. You can draw from your kind voice, your strengths, and your model of courage to help you find your courage. Here are some examples of courageous statements. Add your own to the list.

- This is an opportunity.

- I will not let my phobia win.

- I can tolerate discomfort.

- I am capable of many things.

- I have overcome obstacles in the past.

- I can face my fear head-on.

- I am willing to step outside my comfort zone.

- I choose to think about this differently.

- I can take small steps to reach my goal.

- I will survive.

- Even with discomfort, I can keep going.

- I will not listen to my phobic thoughts.

- I can wait it out.

- I am strong, resilient, and brave.

- My courage will have rewards.

- _____

- _____

- _____

Keep your strengths and your kind, courageous words in mind. Think about how this information can be accessible in your daily life. You might create a collage, write a poem, or record your voice saying the words. You could make a list on your phone or write them on a notecard to carry with you. Whatever form you choose is fine. Find a way to make these statements part of your daily life.

Putting It into Practice

You now know many different ways to challenge your phobic thoughts, but just knowing how is not enough. You actually have to practice this way of thinking in order to get good at it. It might have been easy for you to use your smart brain when you were reading the chapter, but it's much more difficult when you are actually in the situation. It can be hard to think clearly when your false-alarm bell is ringing. So it's important to be proactive and take the time to challenge your phobic thoughts.

1. **Set aside twenty to thirty minutes to focus on your thoughts.**

   Don't do it when you're watching TV, taking a walk, or trying to fall asleep. Sit down with a piece of paper and a pencil (or your computer) and actively work on it. Make it a priority.

2. **Write down all your phobic thoughts and worries.**

   List everything you can think of. Just get it out on paper. This also forces you to be specific and actually put your thoughts into words, since sometimes thoughts are just a jumbled mess in our brains.

3. **Challenge one thought at a time.**

   Identify which phobic thought traps you might be stuck in, then use the challenge questions and statements in this chapter (of which a summary is available for download) to help you reach a more logical, realistic thought. A worksheet and examples are also provided to help you with this process. Feel free to come up with your own too.

4. **Come to a conclusion.**

   The benefit of taking the time to challenge your thoughts is that you end up with some sort of plan. You don't have to keep thinking about the same thing over and over. The next time the thought pops up, remember you've already thought about which path you want to take. It might be to think about the situation differently, to be more accepting, or to increase your self-kindness or courage. Whatever your decision, you will need to work on actively implementing that plan.

5. **Delay new thoughts until next time.**

   Challenging your thoughts on a regular basis allows you to delay new phobic thoughts and worries. If a thought pops into your head while you're watching a movie, you can simply note it and plan to think about it more during your active thinking time. It can wait until a more appropriate moment, one in which you're really focused on thinking about it. Let your free time be your free time.

Challenging My Phobic Thoughts and Worries

Example 1: Quinn

My Phobic Thought or Worry: If I am in a large crowd, there is going to be a disaster.

Phobic Thought Traps

- ☑ Predicting the negative
- ☐ Generalizing
- ☑ Exaggerating the severity
- ☐ Demanding certainty
- ☐ Underestimating abilities

Questions to Consider

Question: How accurate am I when I make predictions?

Answer: I cannot always predict what is going to happen. Many times I have thought there was going to be a disaster, and there wasn't.

Question: Is it possible my views about this have been skewed by the media or rare circumstances?

Answer: I have seen disasters on TV, and they seem to always happen in crowded places. However, the disasters are being reported because they are rare.

Question: Do other people do this without something bad happening to them?

Answer: People do things in crowds all the time. Every day in every city, there are probably large groups of people that get together. Things like sporting events, concerts, museums, and public transportation.

Question: If I can't think of something specific, is there really anything to worry about?

Answer: My phobia is tricking me into worrying about every possible disaster. Maybe I am being overly cautious.

Question: What are the benefits of tolerating my discomfort?

Answer: If I can tolerate my discomfort, I will be able to do more with my friends and family instead of saying I can't go.

Possible Conclusions

More Logical, Realistic Thoughts

People are in large crowds all the time and nothing bad happens to them. The likelihood that a disaster will happen is probably very low. My predictions are usually inaccurate, and I cannot prepare for everything.

Acceptance

I have to accept that risk is a part of life. There are many things in my life I can't control. I can aim to live my life bravely.

Kind and Courageous Statements

Being in crowds is going to be uncomfortable at first, but I have made it through tough times before. If I face my fear head on, I will be following my value of spending more time with my friends and family. I am persistent, and I don't give up!

Challenging My Phobic Thoughts and Worries

Example 2: Harrison

My Phobic Thought or Worry: I always mess up when I have to speak in front of a group.

Phobic Thought Traps

☑ Predicting the negative

☑ Generalizing

☐ Exaggerating the severity

☐ Demanding certainty

☑ Underestimating abilities

Questions to Consider

Question: What evidence do I have for and against this thought?

Answer: I actually have messed up before, but there have been a few times when I did pretty well. I don't really know if other people notice when I mess up. I usually get positive feedback even when I mess up.

Question: Am I generalizing from one past situation to all future situations?

Answer: Just because I messed up before doesn't necessarily mean it will happen every single time I speak in front of a group. It's possible I won't mess up.

Question: How likely is it that this will happen again and again?

Answer: "Always" is probably too general. "Sometimes" might be more realistic.

Question: Have I overcome something like this before?

Answer: Yes, I have messed up before. I was upset when it happened, but then a few people told me I did a really good job. I got through it.

Question: Am I being critical of or kind to myself?

Answer: I'm probably being hard on myself. If someone else made the same mistakes, I wouldn't think it's a big deal. Everyone makes mistakes. I can give it my best effort and that is good enough.

Possible Conclusions

More Logical, Realistic Thoughts

Even though I have made mistakes when speaking in the past, that does not mean it will keep happening. No one speaks perfectly. If I do mess up, I can keep going. People seem to think I do well even if I make mistakes.

Acceptance

If I make a mistake, it's okay. I can't expect myself to be perfect. Even professional newscasters like Brian Williams mess up sometimes.

Kind and Courageous Statements

If I feel nervous when speaking, that's okay. I can tolerate the discomfort and still give a good presentation. People have told me I am a good speaker. This is another opportunity for me to build my skills. I can do it!

Challenging My Phobic Thoughts and Worries

My Phobic Thought or Worry: _____

_____

Phobic Thought Traps

☐   Predicting the negative

☐   Generalizing

☐   Exaggerating the severity

☐   Demanding certainty

☐   Underestimating abilities

Questions to Consider

Question: _____

_____

Answer: _____

_____

_____

Question: _____

_____

Answer: _____

_____

_____

Question: _____

_____

Answer: _____

_____

_____

Question: _____

_____

Answer: _____

_____

_____

Question: _____

_____

Answer: _____

_____

_____

Possible Conclusions

More Logical, Realistic Thoughts

_____

_____

_____

_____

_____

_____

Acceptance

_____

_____

_____

_____

Kind and Courageous Statements

_____

_____

_____

_____

Isn't it amazing how much you can think about your thinking? By having done all this thinking, you've taken such an important step toward overcoming your phobia. Now that you're aware of the phobic thought traps, you can catch yourself and choose another path. You can create change just by opening your mind and thinking more flexibly. This skill will continue to help you in the next chapter, where you'll learn how to accept and cope with your physical and emotional reactions. Keep up the good work!

Chapter 7

Understand and Accept Your Feelings

I suggest that you allow yourself to feel comfortable with your discomfort.

—Lieutenant Jadzia Dax in *Star Trek: Deep Space Nine*

Imagine that you're home alone and your parents said they wouldn't be home until late. After reading your favorite mystery novel in bed, you turn out the light and wait for a movie to load on your computer. You start to think about your soccer game tomorrow and how much you want to beat your rival high school. Then you remember it's probably going to rain. Suddenly, there's a creak in the hallway and then another creak. You freeze. You listen. Your muscles tighten and your heart races. Then your dad opens your bedroom door. You instantly realize no one is breaking into the house. Your dad is home early and just wants to show you his new poster. You yell at him for being so weird and tell him to get out of your room.

Reread this scenario and count how many different emotions came up in such a short period of time. It's very common for people to shift emotions throughout the day or even moment by moment. This chapter will help you become more aware of your emotional reactions, and you'll learn how to work with your emotions instead of against them.

What Are Emotions Good For?

Emotions are hard to define, even for scientists, since they are so complex. Simply, emotions are an individual's naturally occurring response to a situation. This response includes our perceptions of the situation (*I'm afraid someone is breaking into the house*), as well as automatic physical changes in our bodies (*My muscles tense and my heart races*). Ultimately, our emotions influence our behavior (*I freeze and listen*).

Emotions act as signals, cueing us that something has changed in the environment or within us. Either way, our emotions are alerting us to the fact that a response is necessary. Emotions can be quite motivating in this way. We have to take action in order to continue our positive emotions or minimize our negative emotions. As you read in the first chapter, fear is an emotion that gets the body moving in order to avoid danger.

Emotions also help us maintain relationships. Do you ever get sick of your parents asking you over and over questions like "How was your day?" or "How are you doing?" or "Are you feeling okay?" Though it may be annoying, they're trying to understand you better by asking about how you feel. Emotions open the lines of communication with others, whether we're sending signals verbally (with our words) or nonverbally (with our body language or facial expressions).

Emotions also help us understand others on a deeper level and give us clues about how we might want to respond to them. For example, if you knew someone was already scared, would you start telling him stories about a terrible crime? If you knew someone was sad, would you unload all your problems on her? Probably not.

Emotions are different for each person and constantly change throughout the day. Yet they're always present, whether we're paying attention to them or not. The problem is, few people are aware of their regularly shifting emotions. Instead, we tend to pay attention to only one or two extreme emotions. It can be your goal to increase your emotional awareness by identifying what you are feeling and why you are feeling it. The more you understand about your emotions, especially ones related to your phobia, the easier it will be for you to accept them and work through them when they come around.

Name That Emotion

The first step in becoming more aware of your emotions is being able to name how you feel. How good are you at identifying how you feel in the moment? Many people say they often aren't sure how they feel. This is not surprising; in some situations, our emotions take over and make it hard to think. If we're not able to think very clearly, it's hard to identify and name how we're feeling. It probably just seems like a blur.

To start, practice recognizing your emotions when you are *not* in a highly emotional situation. Look at the following situations and consider which emotions you would likely feel. Remember, you may experience several emotions at the same time.

Situation 1:

One of your friends forgets to bring her calculator to school and asks to borrow yours, not realizing that you both have math tests at the same time. You apologize and explain why you can't help her, but when you get to your class, you realize your friend has taken your calculator anyway. You can't complete the problems on your test without your calculator, and you run out of time. When you try to explain to your teacher what happened, she tells you to be more responsible next time. Your friend never apologizes for taking your belongings without asking.

What emotion(s) might you experience? _____

_____

_____

Situation 2:

You've been on the varsity swim team for three years, but you've never made the state team. This year, you're determined to make the team and compete in the championship. You've been training hard all season and find out that you made the team. As you touch the wall after your first race of the meet, you see your name under "first place" on the scoreboard. Your whole team is cheering for you on the sidelines as you hop out of the pool.

What emotion(s) might you experience? _____

_____

_____

Situation 3:

You've been looking forward to going to Yellowstone National Park for a family trip for a few weeks now. The day before the trip, your mother's car breaks down. She takes it to the repair shop, but the mechanic is not sure if it will be fixed in time to drive to Wyoming. The next day, you wake up to find out that the trip won't be happening. Instead, you'll be staying home while many of your friends are on vacation.

What emotion(s) might you experience? _____

_____

_____

Situation 4:

You come home from school to an empty house. You search the house looking for your mom but don't find her. You check the backyard for your dog and can't find him either. When you call your mom, it goes straight to voicemail. You walk next door in hopes of finding out where they are, and your neighbor tells you that your dog went missing earlier in the day and your mom left to search for him hours ago.

What emotion(s) might you experience? _____

_____

_____

Now think about the emotions you experience when faced with the specific situations that trigger your phobia. Your emotional reaction might be a bit different before, during, and after you have contact with your phobia.

Time Period	What Emotion(s) Do You Experience?	How Strong Are These Emotions? (0 = not at all strong, 5 = moderately strong, 10 = very strong)
Before contact with phobic object or situation		0 1 2 3 4 5 6 7 8 9 10
During contact with phobic object or situation		0 1 2 3 4 5 6 7 8 9 10
After contact with phobic object or situation		0 1 2 3 4 5 6 7 8 9 10

Now that you have some idea of which emotions are related to your phobia, work on naming these emotional reactions when you are actually in the situation itself. As discussed earlier, we often experience our phobias as confusing fogs. Instead, try to stop for a second and name your feelings so you can better understand your experience. The list of emotions in chapter 3 can give you some ideas.

What Emotions Feel Like

Another way to help you name your emotions is to think about how they usually feel in your body. This means identifying the physical sensations you experience when you have a certain emotion. For example, some people find their stomachs tighten up when they're worried. Others feel their faces getting hot when they're angry. But not everyone has the same physical experience. To become aware of your physical experience, it's sometimes helpful to mentally scan your body from head to toe to make sure you don't miss any details.

Describe a situation in the past that made you feel angry.

_____

_____

_____

What is your physical experience when you are angry?

_____

_____

_____

Describe a situation in the past that made you feel happy.

_____

_____

_____

What is your physical experience when you are happy?

_____

_____

_____

Describe a situation in the past that made you feel sad.

_____

_____

_____

What is your physical experience when you are sad?

_____

_____

_____

Describe a situation in the past that made you feel afraid.

_____

_____

_____

What is your physical experience when you are afraid?

_____

_____

_____

Now that you know how your body typically feels when you experience certain emotions, these physical sensations can act like clues to help you figure out how you are feeling.

If you are able to recognize your physical clues and emotions early on, you may have a better chance of making a good decision about how you should respond. The earlier you are able to put helpful strategies in place, the quicker you can break up any unhelpful patterns. This early identification will ultimately help you react more positively to certain situations. For example:

Stephanie realized that her body gets tired and she has trouble focusing when she is sad. Last week, when all she wanted to do was stay in her room and sleep for several days in a row, she recognized that her low energy was related to her sadness about her cat passing away. She decided to do something to help improve her mood. She chose to take a walk and call a friend, even though all her body wanted her to do was sleep. But after she got moving a bit, she started to feel more energetic and a little less sad.

What Your Phobia Feels Like

Let's look more specifically at the physical cues commonly associated with phobias. Remember the fight-or-flight response your body activates when it's confronted with danger? The same thing happens when your body is triggered by your phobia or a false alarm. The problem is, your brain focuses only on the scariness of the symptoms, rather than all the useful reasons your body is doing what it's doing.

For example, when your heart starts to beat faster in order to circulate blood to the rest of your body, you actually focus only on the fact that your heart is pounding or racing, which may seem scary in the moment. When your muscles tense to prepare your body for action, you notice shaking or cramping. When your sweat glands work harder to cool you down—no surprise here!—you only focus on the fact that you're sweating. These are some other common symptoms:

- Hyperventilating, shortness of breath, or dizziness

- Sensitivity to light or vision changes

- Stomachaches, nausea, or dry mouth

- Difficulty concentrating on other tasks

- Thirst or lightheadedness

- Numbness, tingling in hands and feet, or chills

Even if we experience the exact same emotion as someone else (like fear), we might feel different physical sensations and focus on different physical symptoms. For example, Daniel and Rachel are both afraid of heights, yet they have very different physical experiences. Sometimes people are even more afraid of the physical symptoms than the actual situation, which is the case for Rachel.

Daniel has a fear of heights. He doesn't like to sit on bleachers, go to higher floors in buildings, or even look out the window in his second-story bedroom. When he's faced with these kinds of situations, he experiences nausea, headaches, and difficulty breathing. Daniel is afraid he'll fall and hurt himself, or won't be able to escape from some potential threat (like a fire) if he isn't on the first floor.

Rachel also has a fear of heights. She doesn't like roller coasters, ropes courses, zip lines, or being close to windows in tall buildings. When she's faced with these kinds of situations, she experiences dizziness and her heart races. Rachel is not necessarily afraid for her safety in these situations; for instance, she isn't worried that the zip line might break. She's more worried about the physical sensations she'll experience, which are very uncomfortable and frightening to her.

Daniel and Rachel both focus on how horrible these symptoms feel in their bodies. Unfortunately, they tend to forget about the purpose of these symptoms and the fact that their bodies are simply reacting to the signals they are given, whether the situation is a real threat or a false alarm.

What physical symptoms do you focus on when you are faced with your phobia or even start to think about your phobia?

_____

_____

_____

_____

_____

The good news is that whether your body is reacting to a real threat or a false alarm, these physical responses are not dangerous. Even though your fight-or-flight response may have been triggered at an unnecessary time, your body can still handle it, and the experience will not last forever. Once the real or perceived threat has passed, levels of hormones in the body decrease, which signals the sympathetic nervous system to slow down and the parasympathetic nervous system to take over. As you know from chapter 1, the parasympathetic nervous system can be thought of as the "off switch" that is responsible for rest and digestion.

We don't really need to figure out how to change your fight-or-flight response, because it's a very important protective tool. Instead, we want to figure out how to decrease the false alarms, or at least make them less scary.

What Your Phobia Feels Like: Practice

In the next few weeks, come back to this page and keep a record of the times you've been able to identify your physical sensations and name your emotions in phobic situations. The more you increase your awareness, the more chances you'll have to create a new pattern.

Date	Situation	Physical Sensations	Emotions I Named	Strength of Emotions
Example: May 2	*My teacher stopped me in the hallway and said she needed to talk to me after school.*	*Tense* *Fast heartbeat* *Sweaty*	• Upset • Nervous • Confused	0 1 2 3 4 5 6 7 8 9 ⑩
				0 1 2 3 4 5 6 7 8 9 10
				0 1 2 3 4 5 6 7 8 9 10
				0 1 2 3 4 5 6 7 8 9 10
				0 1 2 3 4 5 6 7 8 9 10
				0 1 2 3 4 5 6 7 8 9 10

Balance Your Emotions

We're constantly reminded about how important it is to have a balanced diet. Unfortunately, we don't frequently hear about the importance of emotional balance. An influential researcher and psychologist named Marsha Linehan studies emotions and how they affect our lives. In her landmark 1993 book, she talks about how we respond to situations and the goal of creating balance between thoughts and emotions. Dr. Linehan describes three categories, or what she views as parts of the mind, to help illustrate opposite ends of the spectrum and the more balanced middle path.

The reasoning mind:

- Uses logic, facts, and critical thinking to make decisions

- Ignores or does not pay attention to emotions

The emotional mind:

- Uses emotional experiences and urges to react

- Does not choose a response or think things through

The wise mind:

- Combines reasoning and emotional parts

- Considers both logic and consequences as well as emotions and urges

- Acts in your best interest for the long run

Think about what these different parts of the mind might look like in people. Match the following list of characters or real people with the part of the mind they seem to demonstrate the most.

R = reasoning mind   E = emotional mind   W = wise mind

_____ Sherlock Holmes

_____ Dr. John Watson

_____ Bill Gates

_____ Superman

_____ Dr. Who

_____ Sheldon (from *The Big Bang Theory*)

_____ Miley Cyrus

_____ Homer Simpson

_____ Dalai Lama

_____ Hermione Granger (from the Harry Potter series)

_____ Ron Weasley (from the Harry Potter series)

_____ Dumbledore (from the Harry Potter series)

_____ Professor Xavier (from the X-Men series)

_____ Wolverine (from the X-Men series)

_____ The Hulk

_____ Kim Kardashian

_____ Kirk (from the Star Trek series)

_____ Spock (from the Star Trek series)

_____ Yoda (from the Star Wars series)

_____ C3PO (from the Star Wars series)

_____ Han Solo (from the Star Wars series)

_____ Mark Zuckerberg

_____ Justin Bieber

Now consider the positive and negative aspects of each part:

What are some benefits of using the reasoning mind? _____

_____

_____

What are some consequences of using the reasoning mind? _____

_____

_____

What are some benefits of using the emotional mind? _____

_____

_____

What are some consequences of using the emotional mind? _____

_____

_____

What are some benefits of using the wise mind? _____

_____

_____

What are some consequences of using the wise mind? _____

_____

_____

You probably noticed that the reasoning mind and emotional mind both fall short in some way. When we use only one part of the mind, rather than the combination, we end up ignoring an important part of ourselves. Therefore, the best way to go is to use our more balanced wise mind, considering both how we feel and what is logical.

How might this apply to phobias?

When Jared uses his reasoning mind, he works very hard to rationalize or think through what is actually happening in the phobic situation. He conducts research and spouts off statistics. He tries to convince himself that nothing bad will happen and that his phobias are very unrealistic. Jared also ignores how he is feeling about the situation.

When Audrey uses her emotional mind, she feels her physical sensations and emotions very strongly. She believes her intense emotions are dangerous and escape is necessary in order to feel better. When Audrey escapes, she satisfies her urge to avoid the situation and protect herself from danger. She works very hard to make herself feel comfortable. Audrey also ignores logic and facts about the situation.

Colin recognizes his physical sensations and names his emotions. He makes the connection between an instinctual fear response and his current emotions. But rather than escaping, he uses logic to think through the situation. He considers the facts as well as the short- and long-term consequences. Using his wise mind, Colin acknowledges his emotional experience, and applies logic to the situation in order to make a decision in his best interest.

What part of the mind are you using the most when it comes to your phobia?

_____

How might you be able to create more balance between your reasoning and emotional parts in order to become wiser?

_____

_____

_____

Think About Your Emotions

As you learned in the last chapter, sometimes it's helpful to stop and look at how we're thinking about certain situations. We can also use this skill when it comes to our emotions and physical sensations. For example, when John is near bodies of water, his false-alarm bell starts to ring and his fight-or-flight response is triggered. He begins to have these thoughts about his physical sensations and emotions:

- *There is something wrong with my body.*

- *My heart is beating too fast.*

- *This feeling will last forever.*

- *I can't handle feeling this way.*

These kinds of rigid thoughts are likely to lead to increased feelings of panic, anxiety, or fear, as well as increased physical arousal. John is running the STAIRS pattern.

What thoughts do you have about your emotions or physical sensations? These thoughts are probably most present when you are actually in the phobic situation.

_____

_____

_____

_____

You'll need to challenge these automatic thoughts in order to break up the pattern. Do you remember the discussion about thoughts not always being facts? Well, emotions and feelings are not always facts either. We need to interpret our emotions and physical sensations as well. Let's practice this with John's thoughts.

Rigid thought: *There is something wrong with my body.*

Questions to consider:

- Is my body reacting in a way it shouldn't?

- What is it doing that is abnormal?

- What is it doing that is normal?

Flexible thought: *The sensations in my body feel uncomfortable, but this is how my body responds to threats and false alarms like my phobia. This is expected.*

Rigid thought: *My heart is beating too fast.*

Questions to consider:

- What is the purpose of increased heart rates?

- Is this reaction dangerous or normal?

- Do I have any medical evidence to support that it's too fast?

Flexible thought: *My heart is responding instinctively to a perceived threat. Its purpose is to circulate blood faster. This is a normal reaction and it's not dangerous.*

Rigid thought: *This feeling will last forever.*

Questions to consider:

- What do I know about fight-or-flight responses?

- What does my previous experience tell me about what happens with feelings and physical sensations?

- Is "forever" an accurate word or is it a bit extreme?

Flexible thought: *In the moment, it may feel like the feeling will last forever, but I know that feelings and physical sensations are temporary.*

Rigid thought: *I can't handle feeling this way.*

Questions to consider:

- What are my strengths and abilities?

- Have I been able to get through difficult feelings before?

- What would actually happen if I just stayed with this feeling?

Flexible thought: *I'm strong and have made it through uncomfortable feelings before. It's only temporary and won't hurt me.*

These flexible thoughts are not only more realistic but also help reduce the fear and ultimately break up the STAIRS pattern.

For each of your thoughts about emotions and physical sensations, practice asking yourself challenging questions and coming up with some more flexible ways of thinking. If you are having a hard time coming up with questions to consider, look back at chapter 6 for some ideas.

Rigid thought: _____

_____

Questions to consider: _____

_____

_____

_____

_____

Flexible thought: _____

_____

_____

Rigid thought: _____

_____

Questions to consider: _____

_____

_____

_____

_____

Flexible thought: _____

_____

_____

Rigid thought: _____

_____

Questions to consider: _____

_____

_____

_____

_____

Flexible thought: _____

_____

_____

It's hard to do all this critical thinking when you're actually in your phobic situation. That's why it's helpful to think these things through when you're more relaxed. You might also want to have these thoughts readily available when you do find yourself in a phobic situation. You can write them down on notecards or make a list in a notebook or journal. Try to keep them with you so that when a rigid thought pops up, you are able to challenge your thinking right away.

Accept Your Emotions

Our society spreads the myth that we should be comfortable all the time. We should always be winning, entertained, and having fun. Products promise this comfort, from Pillow Pets to iPhones to Snuggies. Society also suggests that we should reduce our discomfort as quickly as possible. If we feel a negative emotion like anger, sadness, or fear, we should do everything we can to make that feeling go away. We're a fast-paced society and we want things to happen—now!

Unfortunately, the messages society spreads are not always accurate or helpful to everyone. (Think of all the diet, teeth-whitening, and plastic surgery commercials you see on TV.) Even more tragic, the attempts we make to feel comfortable and reduce negative emotions often provide only short-lived success or none at all. At times, these attempts even cause more problems in our lives. For example:

> *Tyler is terrified of dogs. When he was very young, a neighbor's large dog would bark every time Tyler went outside. The dog was friendly, but Tyler thought its bark was scary. Even now, he is still afraid. In order to be comfortable and not experience any fear, Tyler decided to go places only if he is 100 percent sure there will be no dogs there. While this solution makes him feel better, it also means he's missing out on a lot of fun activities, like going to the park to play basketball or spending the night at his friend Michael's house.*

Since feeling comfortable all the time is unrealistic, making this a goal might do more harm than good. But what can we do instead?

The answer is *acceptance*, which means accepting that all emotions are normal and okay. It means we all experience emotions that feel good and bad. It does not mean we have to like it, fight it, or give up. It does mean that we have to acknowledge that *this is what is.* We have to be able to make room for all types of feelings and allow them to come and go. Being able to accept an emotion means that we don't need to change it, react to it, or get rid of it right away. Instead, maybe we can just feel it and go with it.

What might you say to yourself to help you accept an emotion?

_____

_____

_____

_____

Another way to increase acceptance is to practice nonjudging. Usually when we feel emotions, we tend to judge our feelings and ourselves, and take these judgments as facts. For example:

> *Tricia starts to feel nervous when her mother tells her she has a dentist appointment. When they get to the dentist's office, she starts to shake, sweat, and cry. Tricia judges her physical symptoms as horrible and calls herself a wimp for not being able to handle going to the dentist. She believes that the dentist's office is the worst thing in the world because it makes her feel so bad and that she should never have to feel this way.*

As you can imagine, Tricia's judgments are not actually helping her feel any better. If anything, they are probably making things worse by feeding into her STAIRS pattern. The judgments are not providing her with any useful information or helping her make the situation any better.

What judgments do you tend to have about your emotions when you are in your phobic situation?

_____

_____

_____

_____

What judgments do you tend to have about yourself or others when you are in your phobic situation?

_____

_____

_____

_____

Once you catch your judgments, the next step is to consider more realistic facts and opinions. This means describing how you feel, in addition to thinking about what is true in the situation. Take a look at Tricia's shift from judgments to nonjudgments:

Target	Judgment	Nonjudging Facts and Opinions
Physical sensations	Horrible Should never feel this way	I feel uncomfortable right now because dentists' offices are hard for me, but it's okay to feel scared sometimes.
Self	Wimp	Everyone has something they are afraid of. The dentist is hard for me, but that doesn't make me weak.
Others	Worst thing in the world	The dentist is only trying to help me have healthy teeth.

Now practice with your own judgments. See if you can move to a more accepting and nonjudging attitude.

Target	Judgment	Nonjudging Facts and Opinions
Physical sensations		
Self		
Others		

To continue practicing these skills, try the following mindfulness exercise. After reading the directions, close your eyes and picture one of these images:

- Clouds or bubbles moving through the sky

- Leaves flowing down a river

- Suitcases or boxes moving on a conveyor belt

As you imagine one of these situations, try to observe your own thoughts and emotions in the present moment as they might move through the image. For example, you might think, *I'm cold*. Picture this thought or the feeling of coldness moving through the sky, or down the river, or along the conveyor belt. Try to observe your thoughts and feelings without any further judgments. Just notice and acknowledge them and then let them pass by. The goal is to practice observing the presence of your thoughts and emotions without becoming overly involved with them. If you happen to make a judgment or get drawn into your thoughts, simply bring your attention back to the present moment. Now set a timer for about five minutes and close your eyes.

The more you practice this skill, the better you'll get. You should first practice in a relaxing setting, and with time your skill will become more automatic. Think of how useful it will be to acknowledge your thoughts and feelings but not have to be overcome by them.

The last skill to help with acceptance is recognizing the connection between emotions and behaviors. People frequently choose their behaviors based on how they feel in the moment rather than on their goals. For example:

Jenna is anxious about the upcoming talent show and believes she can't possibly do schoolwork while she is anxious. Instead, she decides to wait to do her homework until she feels better.

What emotions frequently dictate your behavior?

_____

_____

_____

_____

What things do you often avoid or delay due to your emotions?

_____

_____

_____

_____

Waiting to feel better is very common. Remember our discussion about wanting to feel comfortable all the time? We believe that we can't do things while we're uncomfortable. The fact is, we can. We do a lot of things when we're uncomfortable, like give speeches, ride in airplanes, or go to parties where we don't know anyone.

What are some behaviors or things you do even when you're uncomfortable?

_____

_____

_____

_____

Here's another way to look at it. Let's say that you're very afraid of throwing up, after a bad experience with food poisoning a few years ago; now, every time your stomach feels a little weird, you immediately assume you'll throw up. You just ate a greasy dinner and your anxiety is very high. Your friend calls and asks if you want to go to a movie. You haven't seen your friend in three weeks because she went on a trip to Spain. You decide that you can't go to the movie because you're really nervous about throwing up in the theater. All you want to do is lie down on the couch until your stomach feels better.

In this situation, your mood, especially your anxiety, is deciding what you should do. Now, what if you would get $100 if you went to the movie? Would that change your mind? What about $1,000? Or $10,000?

The point is that we're able to do things even if we aren't in the mood. We're also able to do things even when we feel really bad. Our goals and ambitions don't have to change just because we have uncomfortable emotions. Most importantly, we can accept our anxiety or fear and still move forward.

What are some things you could do (that you normally wouldn't think you could do) even with your uncomfortable emotions?

_____

_____

_____

Work with Your Emotions

Accepting your emotions does not necessarily mean surrendering or giving in to them. You can also take active steps in your everyday life to increase positive emotions. Using this list, check activities you might be able to try, or do more often, to improve your overall mood.

- ☐ Talk to a friend
- ☐ Watch a movie
- ☐ Listen to music
- ☐ Exercise
- ☐ Get fresh air
- ☐ Do something artistic
- ☐ Read
- ☐ Tell someone you love them
- ☐ Play with your pets
- ☐ Drink tea or hot chocolate
- ☐ Write in a journal
- ☐ Smell flowers
- ☐ Practice a magic or card trick
- ☐ Put on lotion
- ☐ Take a shower or bath
- ☐ Make jewelry
- ☐ Ride a bike
- ☐ Draw
- ☐ Take or organize photos

- ☐ Eat your favorite food
- ☐ Go to your favorite restaurant
- ☐ Volunteer
- ☐ Curl up in a soft blanket
- ☐ Go to a comforting place
- ☐ Play a sport
- ☐ Go for a walk or run
- ☐ Go to the park
- ☐ Swim
- ☐ Go to a pet store or zoo
- ☐ Look up funny videos online
- ☐ Watch the sun set
- ☐ Give yourself a manicure
- ☐ Do a random act of kindness
- ☐ Do a puzzle
- ☐ Play video games
- ☐ Go to the beach
- ☐ Build something
- ☐ Spend time with friends

☐ Take a drive

☐ Make a snack for your family or friends

☐ Watch your favorite TV show

☐ Read an inspirational book or quotes

☐ Write a letter

☐ Cook or bake

☐ Search for cute animals online

☐ Do something silly

☐ Dance or sing

☐ Go bowling

☐ Play a board game

☐ Help someone else

☐ Paint

☐ Reach out to someone you miss

☐ Play an instrument

☐ Learn something new

☐ Rearrange your closet or room

☐ Shoot hoops

☐ Take a nap

☐ _____

☐ _____

☐ _____

You might also want to reduce some behaviors or activities that are likely to increase negative emotions. Check any you may need to decrease.

☐ Excessive caffeine intake (soda, coffee, tea, and chocolate)

☐ Excessive sugar intake (desserts, soda, and sweetened cereals)

☐ Excessive artificial sweetener intake (diet sodas or foods)

☐ Excessive salt intake (table salt, salty snack foods, processed foods)

☐ Excessive flour intake (white bread, rolls and buns, white pastas, and pretzels)

☐ Too much food in general

☐ Use of nicotine

☐ Use of drugs or alcohol

☐ Too much sleep

There are also several exercises, or coping skills, specifically designed to calm and relax your body. The goal of relaxation is not to prevent or take away all your fear and discomfort. (Remember from chapter 1 what would happen if you didn't have any fear?) Instead, relaxation exercises can help you tolerate or get through some difficult emotions, sensations, and situations. Plus, you don't need equipment for it—just your body and your brain.

It's usually helpful to try different types of relaxation exercises to see which ones work best for you. Relaxation is also a skill that takes practice. It's difficult to make yourself relax in a stressful situation if you've never practiced relaxing in a less stressful environment. Practice these skills at home first, and then move on to more difficult situations when you're more confident in your skills.

Breathing

When people are scared, stressed, or anxious, they tend to breathe in some pretty unhelpful ways. They may hold their breath, breathe in too much, or take rapid, shallow chest breaths. These types of breathing can throw off the balance of oxygen and carbon dioxide in our bodies, resulting in some physical symptoms like dizziness. Instead, we want to breathe slowly and deeply from our diaphragms. This type of breathing will signal the parasympathetic nervous system to calm the rest of the body.

To practice, lie down on the floor in a comfortable position and breathe naturally. Put one hand on your chest and one hand on your stomach, and notice where you are breathing. Does your chest move up and down, or does your stomach move up and down?

To breathe from your diaphragm, you'll bring in air through your nose, which should make your stomach expand. Think about what happens when you blow up a balloon. When you put air into the balloon, it gets bigger; let air out, and it shrinks. When you breathe out of your mouth, your stomach should go back in, just as the balloon would get smaller. During all this breathing, the hand you have on your chest shouldn't be moving much.

Now practice about five diaphragmatic breaths. Remember to breathe in a normal amount of air. Breathe in for about three seconds and out for about five seconds.

If for some reason you start to feel a little dizzy while doing this exercise, you might be taking in too much air. Go back to your normal breathing, and then try diaphragmatic breathing with two seconds in and four seconds out. Each person's normal breath is a little different. This might feel a little awkward at first, but with practice it will become much easier.

Imagery

It might also be helpful to use your imagination. In this exercise, you should get in a comfortable position, close your eyes, and take three breaths. Then pick a comforting or calming place you would like to imagine. It can be a real place you have been to before or a made-up place, like a castle in the clouds. Spend about ten minutes really exploring your place. To do this, go through your five senses:

- What do you see? Look all around you, close by and far away. Take in all the little details. What objects, colors, and shapes do you see?

- What do you hear? What sounds are in your comforting place? Music, wind, waves?

- What do you smell? Is there newly cut grass or freshly baked bread?

- What do you taste? Is there any food in your comforting place? Or maybe you can taste the air?

- What do you feel? What are you physically touching with your hands or feet? What is the temperature? How are your clothes resting on your body?

- How do you feel in your place? Are you relaxed, calm, or happy?

- How do you feel in the real world? What does your body feel like now that you are relaxed?

Remind yourself that you can go to this place whenever you want to. It's always there. Then take three breaths again and slowly come back to the present moment, feeling relaxed and refreshed.

Grounding

You can also use your five senses to help ground yourself in the present moment. If there is a lot going on around you or if you start to feel out of sorts, you can stop and simply name five things around you in each sensory category. Count them off on your fingers. For example:

- I see a window, a painting of flowers, a water bottle, a computer, and a lamp.

- I hear the air conditioning, a rattling vent, my cat meowing, a car going by, and the TV on downstairs.

- I smell lotion, Mexican food, rain, my cat, and nail polish.

- I taste salt, pepper, cheese, bread, and milk.

- I feel the chair under me, the clothes on my skin, the ring on my finger, the hat on my head, and the computer.

Focusing on details around you can help bring you back to reality and shift your awareness.

Tensing and Relaxing

Have you ever noticed you were tense, but had a hard time just letting the tension go? When it's tough to relax your body, actively tense your muscles and then relax them. You'll be able to feel the difference between full tension and relaxation. You can tense and relax your whole body at once, but sometimes it's better to go slowly through each different muscle group.

Once again, find a comfortable position, close your eyes, and take three breaths. Scan your body for tension. Starting at your feet and moving all the way to the top of your head, squeeze each muscle group for about ten to fifteen seconds (but not so hard that it hurts). While you are squeezing, concentrate on what the tension feels like. Remember to keep breathing. Then release the tension for fifteen to twenty seconds. You might feel a little warmth in your muscles when you relax them. Again, really focus on what it feels like when tension leaves your body.

Here is a list of ways to tense and release different muscle groups from your toes to your head:

- The Bird: curl your toes under like you are trying to stay perched on a branch.

- The Ski Jumper: flex your toes toward your shins to get some good air.

- The Bull Rider: squeeze your knees and thighs together to hang on.

- The Crunch: squeeze your abs like you would in a sit-up.

- The Cat: arch your back to get that good long stretch.

- The Fighter: ball your fists tightly, ready to jab.

- The Flying Squirrel: stretch your arms out to the side as far as you can to glide.

- The Bat: squeeze your shoulder blades together to prepare your wings.

- The Turtle: raise your shoulders to your ears like you are tucking into your shell.

- The Guilty Child: put your chin down and stretch the back of your neck, looking at the ground.

- The Owl: tilt your head back, stretching the front of your flexible neck.

- The Clown: make a really funny face by furrowing your eyebrows, squeezing your eyes tight, squishing your nose, and clenching your teeth.

Exercise

We all know exercise is important because it keeps our bodies strong and healthy. But most people don't realize how vital exercise can be in reducing overall anxiety and stress. Aerobic exercises and relaxed movements, like stretching, help circulate your blood, bring oxygen to your muscles, and release toxins. Exercise also increases the production of helpful endorphins, hormones, and neurotransmitters. So when you are feeling really nervous or tense, you could run around the block or do lots of jumping jacks to help your body get energized and then naturally calm itself down.

Most doctors and scientists suggest exercising from three to five days a week for thirty to forty minutes. You can also practice your breathing while you exercise, as is emphasized in yoga. Taking the time to exercise and stretch your muscles can improve not only your flexibility but also how you feel. Additionally, exercise can help you sleep better and increase your sense of accomplishment and mastery.

Practice Plan

Now that you've learned many new strategies and coping skills, you'll need to make time in your busy schedule for them. This means doing something fun, enjoyable, or comforting every day. It can be big or small. It may mean cutting out some things that aren't so helpful. It also means practicing relaxation exercises to reduce overall tension and to have a tool when you need it to calm down. Set some of your own personal practice goals below.

To increase positive emotions, I will practice this strategy: _____

_____

- Why this strategy is important to me: _____

_____

- Number of days per week I'll practice: _____

- Time of day I'll practice: _____

- Amount of time I'll practice: _____

- What might keep me from practicing: _____

_____

- After a week of practice, this is how I feel about my progress: _____

_____

To decrease negative emotions, I will practice this strategy: _____

_____

- Why this strategy is important to me: _____

_____

- Number of days per week I'll practice: _____

- Time of day I'll practice: _____

- Amount of time I'll practice: _____

- What might keep me from practicing: _____

_____

- After a week of practice, this is how I feel about my progress: _____

_____

If you practice your new skills for four to six weeks, they will likely become habit for you. You might also find an easy way to work them into your schedule. Once you are ready, you can practice with a different skill. And if you find these skills aren't very useful, try some different ones. The most important thing is to keep at it and find strategies that help you work with your emotions.

Now that you've done the work in this chapter do you feel a bit lighter? Isn't it freeing to know you don't have to battle your emotions anymore? Understanding your emotions is a skill you can use for the rest of your life. But most importantly, *accepting* your emotions will help you conquer your phobia. When your focus shifts from having to feel good all the time to following your goals and values no matter how you feel, you'll be in charge instead of your emotions being in charge. In the next chapter, you'll see how phobic thought patterns and emotions lead to safety behaviors. Rather than being ruled by your phobia, you'll learn about brave behaviors you can use to beat it!

Chapter 8

Confront Your Phobia

Each of us must confront our own fears, must come face to face with them.
How we handle our fears will determine where we go with the rest of our lives.
To experience adventure or to be limited by the fear of it.

—Judy Blume, author

Do you remember playing follow-the-leader or Simon Says when you were a little kid? You had to copy the leader or do whatever Simon told you to do or you would be out. While these games were fun, at some point you were probably happy the game was over. Imagine what it would be like if you had to go a day, a week, or even a year copying someone or doing every little thing that person told you to do. And if you didn't do it just right, you would lose!

Well, you might have already realized that your phobia is like Simon. Phobias like to push us around and tell us what to do and what not to do. By using phobic thought patterns, our phobias scare us and ultimately determine our behavior. For example:

When Hunter's phobia repeatedly tells him tall buildings are unsafe and will collapse, he changes his behavior. Instead of going to his favorite rooftop restaurant on the fifty-first floor of a downtown building, he decides to go to a restaurant in a one-story building. Instead of visiting his aunt at her tenth-floor apartment, he asks to meet somewhere else for lunch.

While these changes may not seem like a big deal, they start to add up. Hunter's decisions are based on what his phobia is telling him to do, not necessarily on his values or what he really wants to do. In this chapter, you'll learn more about how we can confront our phobias instead of behaving the way they want us to.

Common Safety Behaviors

In chapter 3, you were introduced to the idea of safety behaviors. In chapter 7, we talked about coping skills, or things people do to help themselves get through difficult emotions, sensations, or situations.

It's understandable that people want to feel better and get back to normal as soon as possible. But safety behaviors are a little different because their whole purpose is to keep someone from feeling any discomfort or to keep something bad from happening. Safety behaviors are actions meant to eliminate negative feelings or possible negative outcomes related to our phobias.

Safety behaviors fall into different categories. Read the examples and see if you can think of another example that would fit in each category. It can be a behavior you've used, a behavior someone else has used, or one you make up.

Avoidance

Completely staying away from something you fear. (You might try to avoid an object, a situation, or even physical sensations.)

- Leah won't see a movie in a movie theater because she believes she could be attacked.

- Jackson hasn't been on a plane since he was five years old because he doesn't like the feeling of turbulence.

- Isabella won't exercise because she thinks she'll have a heart attack.

- _____

  _____

Escape

Leaving a situation as soon as it starts to feel uncomfortable or unsafe. (In a situation where escape is difficult, you might try to get as far away as possible.)

- Diego is willing to ride his bike around the neighborhood, but the second he sees someone walking a dog, he turns the other way and rides home.

- When Violet went on vacation, she tried snorkeling for the first time. When she saw a fish near her, she quickly surfaced and swam back to the boat.

- Jake will attend parties and social functions, but if there are balloons, he'll immediately go to any other room without balloons.

- _____

  _____

Distraction

Purposefully focusing your attention on something else in order to not focus on something fearful; trying to stay busy or occupied as a way of escaping.

- Nora reads the newspaper every day on the subway to keep herself from noticing how many people are crowded into the small space.

- Piper watches TV while she eats to pull her attention away from the food textures in her mouth that might make her gag.

- Grayson plays games on his phone while getting his blood taken so he won't faint.

- _____

  _____

Overprotection

Going above and beyond to make sure you are safe. (Depending on the fear, you may take extreme measures to make sure yourself and possibly others are protected.)

- Henry wears gloves or uses a tissue to protect himself from germs when touching public doors and money.

- Peyton wears long sleeves or covers her arms with her hands to protect the areas where she would get a shot.

- Lisa wears her seatbelt very tightly and grips the armrests to keep herself from getting hurt in case of an accident.

- _____

  _____

Overpreparing

Getting ready or making a plan for the worst-case scenario; working really hard to make sure something bad doesn't happen.

- When Lena enters a building, she looks for the nearest exits so she knows where to go if she needs to leave quickly.

- When Finn drives, he makes sure his car door is unlocked so he can exit the car quickly if he needs to.

- Ben thinks he is going to fail his final exam in geography. Before the exam, he studied for weeks and wrote out the countries and their capitals one hundred times.

- _____

  _____

Checking

Making sure everything is safe or the way it's supposed to be, usually several times.

- Chase constantly calls or texts his parents when he's away from home to make sure the dogs are safe and okay.

- Fatima touches her throat in order to check her pulse and be sure she's not having a heart attack.

- Alice cuts her food into tiny pieces to make sure nothing sharp or dangerous is in it before she eats it.

- _____

Superstitions

Believing your actions will cause something to happen or not happen and behaving accordingly. (The action and the outcome usually have no real connection.)

- Joseph has to have a rock in his right pocket whenever he does any kind of public speaking in order for it to go well.

- Amy will not step on the cracks of the sidewalk because she thinks something bad will happen to her sister if she does.

- Jace has to look in the direction he is traveling on an elevator (up when going up and down when going down) for it to operate correctly.

- _____

Closeness

Requiring people or objects to be close in distance or easily accessible; relying on others or things for safety.

- Evelyn has to have a friend or family member with her when she leaves the house.

- Bruno must have his phone with him at all times just in case he needs to contact someone or someone needs to contact him.

- When Griffin is at a park, he must be able to see his car and get to it quickly in case he needs something from it or has to get away in a hurry.

- _____

Safety Words

Using language to show you are unsure because you don't want to make a mistake or tell a lie; questioning what has actually happened or how you really feel about things, because you want to be certain.

- Rojan told his dad, "I might have done all my work."

- Elizabeth told her mom, "She said I should come in early tomorrow, I think."

- Cooper told his friends, "I will probably play basketball this weekend."

- _____

_____

Reassurance

Asking questions, usually many times, to feel more comfortable; wanting to hear from others that everything is going to be okay.

- When Ahmet goes outside, he asks anyone who's around if there are snakes.

- Before every meal, Ryan asks his friends or family if the food is fully cooked because he's afraid of getting sick.

- Emma's boyfriend promises her every day that she does not have cancer.

- _____

_____

Accommodation

Having others do things for you because of your fear. (You may ask people to do things or they may offer because they know it's hard for you.)

- Camden asks his sister to trade chores. He offers to wash the dishes if she'll pick weeds from the garden because he doesn't want to be near any insects.

- Lexi asks her friend to come over because she doesn't want to leave her house when the weather looks bad outside.

- Julia's mom drives the longer way to school because she knows Julia doesn't want to go by the house of an old woman who scares her.

- _____

_____

Which Safety Behaviors Do You Use?

Think about how you act when you are confronted by your phobia or think you might have to face your phobia. What does your phobia tell you to do? And how do you respond?

Check the safety behaviors you use, and describe what you do to try to stay safe. Be as specific as possible. You might have more than one safety behavior in the same category. Look back at the definitions and examples to help you remember each category.

☐ Avoidance

_____

_____

_____

☐ Escape

_____

_____

_____

☐ Distraction

_____

_____

_____

☐ Overprotection

_____

_____

_____

☐ Overpreparing

_____

_____

_____

☐ Checking

_____

_____

_____

☐ Superstitions

_____

_____

_____

☐ Closeness

_____

_____

_____

☐ Safety words

_____

_____

_____

☐ Reassurance

_____

_____

_____

☐ Accommodation

_____

_____

_____

Why do you do these behaviors? How are they helpful?

_____

_____

_____

_____

Why We Repeat Safety Behaviors

To better understand why we use safety behaviors, you need to know a little about reinforcement. When a behavior is reinforced, we continue to repeat the behavior. There are two main reinforcement patterns. First, positive reinforcement is when we continue to repeat a behavior to earn some type of reward. For example, Xavier continues to mow the lawn every week so he can earn money.

Behavior → Add Reward → Continued Behavior

Mow the lawn → Earn money → Mow the lawn again next week

Second, negative reinforcement is when we continue to repeat a behavior to reduce some type of negative experience. For example, Bill continues to wear earplugs at rock concerts so his ears won't hurt from the loud music.

Behavior → Reduce Negative Experience → Continued Behavior

Wear earplugs → Ears don't hurt → Wear earplugs at next concert

Safety behaviors are examples of negative reinforcement. For instance, Hunter realized if he stays away from tall buildings, his level of discomfort decreases. Since staying away seemed to work, he will keep doing it in the future. To Hunter, it makes total sense.

Safety Behavior → Decrease Discomfort → More Safety Behaviors

Avoid tall buildings → Don't have to feel discomfort → Continue to avoid tall buildings

Once we figure out a safety behavior that seems to work for us, it's very likely we'll keep doing it, mostly because it feels better than not doing it. Unfortunately, safety behaviors are part of the STAIRS pattern that keeps our phobias going. Keep reading to find out how.

Isn't Safety a Good Thing?

The short answer is yes. It's probably one of the first things your parents taught you: "Look both ways before you cross the street" and "Don't touch the stove." We all follow rules and take precautions in order to stay safe. When you look at the safety behaviors we just listed and their effects, they seem to make sense. It may take a little extra effort or time to do them, but in general, these behaviors don't seem like a big deal. And they aren't, especially when they are used every once in a while.

But here comes the problem.

People with phobias rely on safety behaviors. We come to feel like we *need* safety behaviors to survive, and we overuse them. The safety behaviors help us feel in control and think everything will go smoothly. But what happens when we can't use a safety behavior? Think about it.

How is Jackson (who has avoided planes since he was five) going to feel when he wants to visit a college in California, but he has to get on a plane to do it? How is Ryan (who wants reassurance) going to feel when his family says they are no longer going to answer his questions about food preparation? How is Ben (who overprepares) going to feel when he sees a question on his final exam that he didn't prepare for?

Since we can't control everything, sooner or later, we will come across a situation when we can't use safety behaviors. Then what?

Look back at your list of safety behaviors. How would you feel if you were confronted with your phobia and could *not* use your safety behaviors?

_____

_____

Since you probably listed some type of negative feelings, this shows us that safety behaviors don't actually fix our phobias. We know safety behaviors make us feel better in the moment, but they are only a short-term fix. Each time you have contact with your phobia, you have to continue using your safety behaviors in order to get through it. Ultimately, safety behaviors don't help you conquer your phobia; they keep the STAIRS pattern going and even make it stronger. And here's how:

- Safety behaviors don't allow you to have real contact with your phobia.
- They don't allow you to correct phobic thought patterns.
- They support false alarms.
- They don't allow you to learn how to cope with situations.
- They make you feel like you can't handle situations without them.
- They work only in the short run.
- They get you stuck in a repetitive cycle.

How do your safety behaviors get in the way? How are they holding you back?

_____

_____

_____

Now you might be wondering, if safety behaviors aren't the answer, then how do you conquer your phobia? Instead of focusing on the short-term goal of decreasing discomfort as soon as possible (which is why we use safety behaviors), we want to shift our focus to the long-term goal of facing our phobia. This means having a direct experience with our phobia, learning from it, tolerating our feelings, and coping through it. In order to shift our thinking from a real threat to false alarm, we have to experience our phobia in a different way. We have to learn that safety behaviors are not actually necessary and we can survive without them. The only way to learn that there is no danger is to actually find out what happens without our extra safeties and precautions. Then we can start to see the truth.

Picture this scenario. You are invited to a friend's house to go swimming in his new pool. You know how to swim, but you've never been in this pool before. So you bring along a life jacket and wear it while you go swimming.

What does the life jacket represent? _____

_____

Why might you have a life jacket on? _____

_____

What do you think would happen if you chose to take your life jacket off? _____

_____

When facing our phobia, the ultimate goal is to approach our phobic situations and triggers in order to learn more. When we use safety behaviors, we're listening to our phobia, which is telling us the situation is dangerous and we have to protect ourselves. When we face our phobia without safety behaviors, we have the opportunity to learn that the situation might not be as dangerous as we thought. Then the safety behaviors become a waste of time and energy, because they aren't necessary. In false-alarm situations, safety behaviors don't prevent danger or keep us safe because there isn't a real threat to begin with.

Replacing Safety Behaviors

You might be wondering how you can possibly get through life without your safety behaviors. Since you've relied on them to keep you safe, it may feel really scary to face the world without them. When you think about not using your safety behaviors, instead of seeing it as a loss, treat it as an opportunity to discover new behaviors that will help you conquer your phobia and will be more beneficial for you in the long term. Shift your thinking from:

Stopping Safety Behaviors → Starting Brave Behaviors

In order to start brave behaviors, you'll have to think about your current safety behaviors and possible replacements for those behaviors. You don't want the replacement to be just another safety behavior, because that wouldn't do much good. A better alternative would be to move toward coping skills. But what's the difference between safety behaviors and coping skills?

Safety Behaviors	Coping Skills
We create distance from phobic situations.	We engage with phobic situations.
We believe there is a real threat.	We recognize there is a false alarm.
We stay on high alert for danger.	We validate feelings of discomfort as normal.
We increase worry and preparation.	We increase learning and acceptance.
We demand comfort immediately.	We tolerate discomfort and wait it out.
We have low confidence in our ability to handle hard things.	We have high confidence in our ability to handle hard things.

Let's go back to Hunter and his phobia of heights. He was definitely using safety behaviors like avoidance and overpreparing. He kept himself from going into any buildings more than two stories high. At the same time, he was always cautious and prepared for the worst-case scenario when it came to tall buildings. He would even plan his walking and driving paths so he would not have to go near tall buildings. For Hunter to move from safety behaviors to brave behaviors, he will have to replace his usual behaviors with new coping skills.

Current Safety Behaviors	Alternative Coping Skills
• Avoid favorite restaurant • Avoid aunt's apartment • Avoid going into building over two stories high • Plan routes away from tall buildings	• Challenge phobic thought patterns about tall buildings • Be willing to go near and into tall buildings • Tolerate and accept discomfort • Breathe and ground myself when facing fears • Have pictures of family and friends as a reminder of values

Remember, coping skills are meant to help us tolerate or get through difficult emotions, sensations, or situations. They help us face what is difficult and come out on the other side, rather than remove all the discomfort. Let's try another one.

Ever since Ryan heard about nine people in his town getting food poisoning from a local restaurant, he's been very fearful of getting sick. He worries about all the food he eats and how it might affect him. He even asks if foods that can be eaten raw, like broccoli, are cooked enough. Ryan uses overprotection, checking, reassurance, and accommodation to make sure he is completely safe.

Current Safety Behaviors	Alternative Coping Skills
• Cook own food as much as possible • Inspect food before eating • Ask if food is fully cooked • Have others try food first	• Challenge phobic thought patterns about food poisoning • Be willing to eat without 100 percent certainty • Take my best guess • Tolerate and accept discomfort • Exercise and practice imagery for overall mood

It can also be very tempting to rely on others to help us through hard situations. Support from others is great, but you have to make sure the support is not functioning as a safety behavior. You have to ask yourself if the type of support you are requesting is feeding into your phobic pattern. Use the following questions to help you decide whether your supports are actually safety behaviors.

- Do I require constant closeness when I'm in my phobic situation?

- Do I have rigid rules about not being left alone?

- Do I struggle to do things independently?

- Do I ask the same questions over and over?

- Do I ask questions to feel less anxious?

- Do I ask questions that can't really be answered with certainty?

- Do I ask questions already knowing the answer I want to hear?

- Do I ask others to do things for me so I don't have to feel uncomfortable?

- Do I have rigid rules I want others to live by so I feel better?

Is support from others serving as a safety behavior in your life? Give examples.

_____

_____

_____

_____

The reason these types of support are not very helpful is because they decrease your ability to conquer your phobia and build up your own coping skills. So what kind of support would be more helpful?

Support that does not act as a safety behavior includes *validation, boundaries,* and *encouragement.* When others validate you, they understand how you are feeling. They empathize and identify with your situation. For example, Hunter's aunt might validate his experience by saying, "I know this is really scary for you and it's okay to have those feelings," or "I see you're hesitant to take the next step; I get that." Often we just need to know that someone understands what we're going through. We need to hear that it's okay to feel the way we're feeling.

Boundaries are limits we set on behaviors. They are meant to be helpful and to support your goals, not to be punishments. Other people, especially your family, might need to stop some of their accommodating behaviors. Boundaries need to be set around what types of questions they are willing to answer or what rules they are willing to follow. For example, Hunter and his aunt might decide it would be better if she were not willing to go somewhere else for lunch. In order for him to see her, he'll have to come to the apartment. Although this might be hard for him, this boundary helps him get closer to conquering his phobia instead of avoiding it.

You can also get support through encouragement from others. Rather than asking others to reassure or accommodate you, it would be more helpful if they encouraged your logic, flexibility, tolerance, acceptance, and bravery. Ask others to support your goal to conquer your fear, not your avoidance. For example, when Hunter attempts to go to his aunt's apartment, she could say, "You are so brave for taking this on," "You can do it," or "You can beat the fear."

These kinds of messages are much more supportive than someone promising you things they can't really promise, doing things for you, or allowing avoidance to continue. After you think about the support you receive as well as how it affects your phobia, you might want to talk with the people in your support system. They may need a little coaching on distinguishing between what kind of support maintains your phobia and what kind of support helps you conquer your phobia. You can download a handout to share with them at the website for this book (as well as a full-scale version of the exercise below). The more others know about your new coping skills, the more they can help you practice and support you in the right way.

List your current safety behaviors and brainstorm possible alternative coping skills to help you manage your fear, but not run from it.

Current Safety Behaviors	Alternative Coping Skills
• _____	• _____
_____	_____
_____	_____
• _____	• _____
_____	_____
_____	_____
• _____	• _____
_____	_____
_____	_____
• _____	• _____
_____	_____
_____	_____

There is one last thing to know about safety behaviors. Sometimes we find really useful coping skills, but they accidentally turn into safety behaviors. We overuse or rely too heavily on our new coping skills and start to feel like we have to use them in order to face our phobias. So be aware and make sure your new coping skills continue to support your goals and values.

Choose Brave Behaviors

To overcome phobias, we have to change our behaviors. You have already learned how to replace your safety behaviors with new coping skills. The next step is to actually put it all into action, which is called exposure. Exposure exercises require a number of brave behaviors:

- Facing a fear head-on

- Stepping away from safety behaviors

- Using new coping skills

Stop to think for a minute. Why do you have to directly face your fear?

_____

_____

_____

_____

It's all about learning. When your phobia was developing, you were doing a lot of observing and learning, but you learned the wrong information. When we practice exposures, it's all about relearning. We have to figure out what is true, what is real, what we can handle, and what happens. You can't learn these things by hiding in your bedroom. You have to be brave and explore. Did you learn how to ride a bike by reading about it in a book? Did you learn how to swim by watching the Olympics on TV? No, you had to go do it!

Exposures allow you to put all your new skills into practice, like having a new conversation with your thoughts, understanding and accepting your feelings, and replacing safety behaviors. Exposures also strengthen these skills.

When you face your fear, you are gathering evidence to help you decide whether your automatic interpretations are true. For example, if Hunter faces his fear and goes into a tall building, he can see which of his thoughts are accurate. Since he will most likely get in and out of the building without any disasters, he can start to change his phobic thoughts about tall buildings collapsing if he enters them. Exposures help us learn whether the connections we made in the past and continue to carry around with us are accurate. This new learning will lead to more flexible and realistic thinking.

Exposures also allow us to practice managing our physical and emotional responses to a situation. It's easy to talk about tolerating and accepting an emotion. It's a lot harder to actually do it. When we face our fears, we trust that something called *habituation* will happen. Habituation basically means that with time and repeated practice, our brains and bodies will adjust and get used to the situation.

Name some situations you have been in that were hard or uncomfortable at first, but you got used to after a while.

_____

_____

_____

Some typical examples include getting used to certain foods, amusement park rides, and cold water in a pool or the ocean. In each of these situations, we might be really uncomfortable at first, but with time, our brains and bodies adjust and it doesn't seem so bad anymore. Sometimes we even start to like it!

Another great example is astronauts. They spend years preparing to go into space. They perform zero gravity exposures, which means they train underwater for hours in their space suits to adapt to weightlessness. They also spin in a human centrifuge meant to prepare them for the very high g-forces during takeoff. These experiences may sound like fun, but they're actually very challenging and uncomfortable.

Astronauts expose themselves to these situations so they can learn how to handle similar conditions in space, as well as learn how to tolerate their physical and emotional responses.

Exposures are the same kind of training for your brain and body. Just like learning a new skill, exposure training can be challenging and uncomfortable at first. But as you keep practicing, it will get easier and easier.

Describe a type of training you have gone through; for example, maybe you learned a new sport or how to play musical instrument.

_____

_____

_____

So why do astronauts, athletes, and musicians put themselves through so much hard work and discomfort? It's because they are following their values and goals. And they are willing to put in the time, energy, and effort to reach these goals. They are willing to feel tired, sore, and even nauseated. All over the world, people with different jobs, resources, and abilities are willing to feel uncomfortable in the short run in order to get what they want in the long run. It has been said that the best things in life are not free; it takes work to get there.

Think about how you would handle this situation:

You find a small kitten stuck in a bush full of thorns near your house. The kitten is crying and squealing, and you know it's in pain. It finally wiggles its way out of the bush. But when you go to pick it up, you notice it has several thorns stuck in its paws. It lies on the ground and can't walk because of the thorns. Every time you get near the kitten, it cries because it doesn't want you to touch it. Now you have a choice. You can either put the kitten through a lot more pain and try to take out the thorns, or you can leave the kitten alone and not cause it any further pain.

What would you do? _____

_____

Now think of yourself as the kitten and the thorns as the phobia that is holding you back. Sometimes we have to go through something painful or uncomfortable in the present in order to experience the benefits later. It's really going to hurt to have those thorns taken out, but it's the only way to get better. We have to tolerate and work through the difficult feelings in order to continue moving toward our goals.

When we practice exposures, we not only start to see some of the benefits of being free from our phobias, but we also get to learn how capable and strong we really are. We can see our ability to tolerate hard situations and not-so-fun feelings. We can see our strength and build up our confidence. Exposures also show us we don't need those safety behaviors anymore, because we're doing just fine without them. We can choose brave behaviors instead. Exposures teach us we can face our fears head-on. This can seem really scary. But once you try it, you realize you can do it! You can take it on.

Summarize for yourself what you can learn from facing your fear.

_____

_____

_____

_____

_____

_____

_____

_____

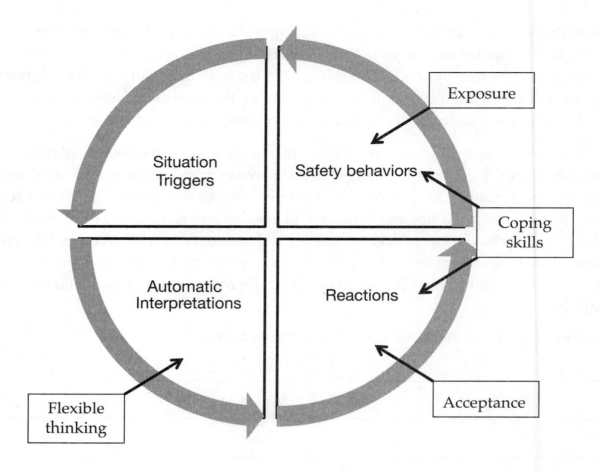

You made it! You now know the key strategies to help you FACE your phobia.

Hopefully you've been practicing some of your new thinking and coping skills along the way. But you might be wondering how exposures actually work. In chapter 9, you'll make a plan for your exposures and put your brave behaviors into action. The more you practice and learn, the more change you can create.

Chapter 9

Experiment with Brave Behaviors

Expose yourself to your deepest fear; after that, fear has no power.

—Jim Morrison, lead singer of The Doors

You learned in chapter 8 about one of the most essential steps of conquering your phobia. Exposure exercises bring together all the strategies and skills you've learned in this book. When you practice exposures, you have to use flexible thinking, accept your physical and emotional reactions, and replace safety behaviors with coping skills. Most importantly, you have to face your fear. These are all new, brave behaviors that will help you beat your phobia. But you probably have a lot of questions about how to actually practice exposure exercises. This chapter will explain the process of planning and implementing your brave behaviors.

The Planning Stage

Like many things in life, exposure exercises require some planning before you actually start practicing. In this chapter, we're going to think of exposure exercises as an experiment in science class. Before you do anything, you first need a plan. In school, you might read instructions from a textbook or listen to the teacher, but here you're going to create your own plan.

Choose Your Topic

In order to decide what you'll be experimenting with, think back to the situations and triggers of your phobia. The topic and content of your experiment should be any situations or triggers that activate your phobia pattern. Remember, it might be a specific situation, such as getting shots; a thought, such as *I need to count to twelve or something bad might happen*; or a physical sensation, such as feeling lightheaded. If you have more than one area to work on, you'll have to conduct a separate experiment for each topic.

Write down your phobia experiment topic here:

_____

_____

_____

Outline Your Steps

Next, you'll need to brainstorm possible steps to help you face your fear. You get to decide how many steps there will be. You can take small steps and gradually move from easier to harder tasks. (Check out the movie *What About Bob?* for a funny view of exposures using baby steps.) You can also jump right in and tackle difficult situations right away. It's up to you. Either way, you should have a plan.

Coming up with your steps requires some creativity. When you brainstorm, write down your ideas on separate slips of paper, sticky notes, or notecards, or use your computer. You want to be able to move the information around so you can put the steps in an order that makes sense for you. This is *your* plan.

Think about what you could do to face your fear. Sometimes it means doing the exact opposite of what your fear is telling you to do. Remember, the only way to conquer a phobia is to actually interact with it.

Try to write down specific action steps. This means focusing on tasks you *can do*, rather than what *not to do*.

Specific action step: Touch coins with my bare hands.

versus

General inaction: Don't wear my gloves.

Specific action step: Look over edge of three-story parking structure.

versus

General inaction: Don't close my eyes when I'm up high.

Depending on your topic, the steps can look very different. When you face situations, it's best if you can work up to having direct contact with your phobia. This might involve getting a shot, holding a snake, driving through a tunnel, or standing in a large crowd at a concert. You'll have to think about smaller steps you can take to help you get closer and closer to your goal. There are many different variables you can consider when you are brainstorming your steps:

- Who you're with

- What time of day it is

- How far away you are from something

- How big an object or place is

You might have steps that look very similar, but one small part is different:

- Riding an elevator to the second floor

- Riding an elevator to the tenth floor

- Riding an elevator alone

- Riding an elevator with others

As you can see, there can be many variations. If a small detail makes the situation easier or harder, you can create separate steps.

Unfortunately, it can be challenging to gain direct access to some phobic situations. You have to consider what you can realistically practice. If you have a fear of flying and conveniently have an uncle who owns his own plane, then you might have easy opportunities for practice. But for those who aren't so lucky, it's going to be much harder to practice with planes. Depending on your phobic situation, you might have to do some creative planning and use as many connections and resources as possible. If you tell people that you're working on conquering your phobia, most will be willing to help you if they can.

You also have access to an enormous amount of content on the Internet. Search Google or YouTube for pictures, stories, or videos on your topic; looking at this information could be one of your exposure steps. These sites are great resources, especially when you don't have easy access to your phobia. Additionally, your exposure practice might include role-playing or imagining certain situations in as much detail as possible.

You can take similar steps when facing triggering thoughts. Rather than getting closer and closer to a certain situation, you'll want to practice having more and more contact with your thoughts about that situation. It might seem strange to have more contact with the thoughts that are bothering you, but remember that facing your fear is what helps you adjust and work through it. If you spend a lot of time exposing yourself to your thoughts, sooner or later they'll actually get boring. Or the thoughts will start to seem silly because you have heard them so much. Depending on your thoughts, you might be able to find some helpful content online. For example, if you had thoughts about getting an illness, you could read articles about the illness or imagine what might happen if you actually had the illness. Other ideas would be to write down your phobic thoughts over and over or to create a recording of your thoughts and listen to it repeatedly.

Ways to Expose Yourself to Phobic Situations and Thoughts

- Have direct contact with your phobia.

- Take small steps to get closer and closer to your phobia.

- Do Internet searches via Google or YouTube.

- View pictures and videos.

- Read books and articles.

- Role-play.

- Imagine the situation in your mind.

- Think thoughts on purpose.

- Put your thoughts on paper.

- Make an audio recording of your thoughts.

When a physical sensation, like your heart beating really fast, starts the whole pattern, you have to find a way to expose yourself to that same physical feeling. Bringing on the physical sensation on purpose allows you to practice with it when you are expecting it, rather than it being a surprise. Your brain also adjusts to the feeling, and you get to see whether the physical sensations are actually threatening. You are training your body and brain to get through it and get used to it.

Here are some ideas to help you replicate these physical sensations.

Physical Sensation	Exposure Ideas
Rapid heart rate	Run in place. Do any aerobic exercise. Drink caffeine. Play video games with movement.

Shortness of breath and difficulty breathing	Climb several flights of stairs.
	Plug your nose and breathe through a straw or coffee stirrer.
	Sit in a car without rolling down the windows.
	Go snorkeling.
Dizziness	Turn in circles really fast.
	Look to the right and left repeatedly.
	Spin in a chair or on a swing.
	Jump on a trampoline.
Lightheadedness	Blow up balloons or inflatables.
	Breathe rapidly to hyperventilate.
	Bend over and hang your head, then sit up quickly.
	Hang upside down on a bar or swing.
	Go on amusement park rides.
Feeling hot or sweaty	Sit or walk outside when it's hot.
	Take a hot shower with the bathroom windows and doors closed.
	Sit in a sauna or hot tub.
	Eat something spicy.
Tension or shaking	Tense muscles in different parts of your body.
	Hold something heavy for a long period of time.
	Hold yoga poses that require strength.
	Do a lot of sit-ups or push-ups.

Physical Sensation	Exposure Ideas
Nausea	Eat a heavy meal. Eat until you feel stuffed. Read while sitting in a car. Smell something you don't like.
Choking or gagging	Hold water in your mouth for as long as you can. Brush the very back of your tongue with your toothbrush. Swallow tiny breath mints or vitamins.
Dry mouth	Put cotton balls inside your cheeks. Swallow a small amount of cinnamon. Eat a lot of crackers without taking a drink. Swallow repeatedly.
Unreality (feeling unreal or like objects around you are unreal)	Stare in the mirror. Stare closely at an object. Wear 3-D glasses.

Some of these ideas might work great for you, and with some you might not feel anything at all. You'll have to try a few different things until you find something that feels similar to the physical sensation you fear. You can also try the exposures at home first and then try them in situations that might be more difficult (like in public).

Remember, safety is important. It's a good idea to practice physical exposure exercises with another person. You also have to consider your general health to decide whether the exposure exercise is okay for you. For example, someone with a medically diagnosed heart condition shouldn't do anything that might make the condition worse. If you are unsure, talk with a parent or medical health professional about what seems reasonable.

Once you have a good list of ideas for exposures, put them in order from easiest to hardest. Look at each of your exposure ideas individually and ask yourself this question: *How hard would it be for me to complete this exposure without using any safety behaviors?*

0	1	2	3	4	5	6	7	8	9	10
Easy					Medium					Hard

Take your best guess and assign a number from the scale above to each exposure exercise. When you put your exposures in order, you'll have an exposure to-do list. As you do this, you might realize you have some gaps to fill in. If you have a lot of exercises that are easy and hard, but nothing in the middle, you might want to brainstorm some more ideas to fill in the gap. Add in as many steps as you like.

Also, make sure you don't leave something out just because it seems too scary. You might not feel like you can do the hard exposures now, but with practice you can slowly work your way up to them. It's a good idea to push the limits as far as you possibly can. This means going above and beyond the fear, and maybe even doing some things people wouldn't do in everyday life; for example, having someone lock you in a closet if you are claustrophobic.

If you go as far as you can and something comes up unexpectedly or if your phobia tries to find a way to worm its way in, you'll be more than ready for it. So even though you might not feel like it's normal or necessary to make snow angels on the bathroom floor, it will definitely help you beat your phobia of germs.

With all this in mind, get a little crazy. Keep asking yourself, *What can I do to conquer my phobia? How can I push myself further? What would make the situation even scarier?* If you can do really hard and uncomfortable things, you can do just about anything.

Here are some examples of exposure outlines or to-do lists. Using the sample topics, steps were brainstormed and then put in order from easiest to hardest. You'll see that some steps are assigned the same number because they're at a similar level of difficulty. Some numbers are skipped if there doesn't seem to be an exposure at that level. Remember, there is no right or wrong way to create your list. Even people with the same phobia might have different exposure steps. It's all about making a plan that works for you.

Phobia Experiment Topic: Getting shots

My Rating	Specific Action Steps
1	Look at pictures of needles.
2	Look at pictures of people getting shots.
3	Watch videos of people getting shots.
4	Drive by the doctor's office and look at the doors. Look at real needles on a table or when someone else is holding them.
5	Watch a syringe being filled.
6	Hold needles in my hands. Sit in the waiting room at the doctor's office.
7	Touch the tip of a needle to my skin by myself. Sit in an exam room at the doctor's office.
8	Let someone else put the tip of the needle to my skin. Watch someone else get a shot.
9	Go to the doctor's office and have my finger pricked.
10	Go to the doctor's office and get a shot.

Phobia Experiment Topic: Thinking I need to count to twelve or something bad might happen

My Rating	Specific Action Steps
2	Look at images of many different numbers.
4	Count to random numbers.
5	Imagine bad things that might happen if I don't count.
6	When I have the urge to count to twelve, count to ten instead.
7	When I have the urge to count to twelve, count to one instead.
8	Make and listen to a recording about the bad things that might happen if I don't count.
9	Have someone tell me to count to twelve, then use coping skills rather than counting.
10	When I have the urge to count to twelve, use coping skills rather than counting.

Phobia Experiment Topic: Feeling lightheaded

My Rating	Specific Action Steps
1	Breathe quickly for one minute.
2	Breathe quickly for three minutes.
3	Hang my head and sit up quickly; repeat.
4	Blow up regular balloons.
5	Blow up a pool raft.
6	Spin around with my head down.
7	Hang upside down on a bar.
8	Hang upside down on a moving swing.
9	Go on a small waterslide.
10	Go on a big waterslide.

Now it's time for you to practice. See if you can come up with steps that would help someone conquer their fear of being outside alone.

Phobia Experiment Topic: Being outside alone

My Rating	Specific Action Steps

Finally, after brainstorming steps and assigning a level of difficulty to each step, complete your own exposure outline.

Phobia Experiment Topic:

My Rating	Specific Action Steps

State Your Hypothesis

When developing a hypothesis, scientists think about the purpose of their experiment and what they are trying to discover or explore. Then they make an educated guess about what they think will happen, based on their knowledge up to this point. Most hypotheses are described as "if...then" statements:

- If tomatoes receive sunlight, then they will grow bigger than tomatoes that don't receive sunlight.

- If someone is left alone in a room with a box labeled "do not open," then they will open it.

Remember, a hypothesis is a guess; the whole point of doing an experiment is to find out whether your hypothesis is true. Many scientists' hypotheses have been wrong, but it's all about learning and seeing what actually happens.

When coming up with your hypothesis, you have two choices: you can base it on your phobic thought patterns, or you can base it on your new, smart, scientific thought patterns. Either way, you'll experiment and get to the truth.

Use these sample hypotheses to help you create your own. Your hypothesis can be related generally to your topic or more specifically to the experiment step you are currently working on.

Phobia Experiment Topic: Getting shots

Phobic Hypothesis: If a needle touches my skin, I will pass out.

Smart Hypothesis: If a needle touches my skin, I will be uncomfortable at first, but then my body will calm down as I adjust.

Phobia Experiment Topic: Thinking I need to count to twelve or something bad might happen

Phobic Hypothesis: If I don't count to twelve, someone I love will get hurt that day.

Smart Hypothesis: If I don't count to twelve, I can still have a good day.

Phobia Experiment Topic: Feeling lightheaded

Phobic Hypothesis: If I feel lightheaded, I will faint and have to go to the hospital.

Smart Hypothesis: If I feel lightheaded, I can tolerate the feeling and keep going.

My Phobia Experiment Topic: _____

My Hypothesis: _____

_____

_____

Gather Your Tools

Before you can experiment, you'll need to gather all the materials for your experiment. You might need to collect or buy supplies (like needles or straws for breathing) or make arrangements to get access to certain objects or places (like snakes or doctors' offices).

You also need to gather up all your new FACE skills and get pumped up to face your phobia. Review your smart, flexible thoughts, and have them easily accessible in case you need them during the experiment. Prepare yourself to accept the discomfort you may feel during the exposure, remembering that it will not last forever and you can handle it. Decide which alternative coping skills you'll use instead of your safety behaviors. Focus on your bravery and willingness to do something challenging in order to beat your phobia.

Lastly, remind yourself why you are doing all this. Go back to your values and goals. Give yourself a pep talk. You get to be in charge when you shift your mind from "I hate this" to "I want to do this." Approach your phobia with courage and determination.

The Action Stage

You are finally there. It's time to go for it. It's time to experiment with exposures and see what happens. It's okay if you're scared—taking the first step is hard. Think about a time when you wanted to do something that was a little scary, like jumping off the high diving board or going zip-lining for the first time. You might have stood there for a long time thinking about it and getting more and more nervous. But sooner or later, you just went for it. And it was okay, maybe even fun. In order to learn, you have to jump in and do it.

Conduct Your Experiment

When you do your exposure experiments, make sure you pay attention to what is actually happening in the moment. A true exposure means being present, without moving away from what you experience or distracting yourself during it. It might be helpful to talk out loud about what you're experiencing. You can talk about your thoughts, what you see in your environment, or what you feel in your body. Just notice what is going on and embrace it.

You can also use a scale to track your fear or discomfort level throughout the exposure, ranking it from 0 (none) to 10 (extremely high).

These ratings will help you decide when to stop your exposure. First, think back to times when you previously interacted with your phobia. Most people report low fear when they are away from their phobia, medium fear right before they interact with their phobia, and high fear when they are face-to-face with it. Once their fear level gets too high, they usually leave the situation.

When practicing exposures, the goal is to stay with it. Stay in the situation until your brain and body have the chance to adjust and naturally calm down. It's expected that your fear level will increase when you practice. We know your false alarm will go off, and that's okay. Since you expect it, you can tolerate it and talk yourself through it instead of escaping right away. This means you shouldn't stop your exposure until your fear level has started to go back down, usually between the low and medium level if possible. Then you can leave the situation feeling more in control rather than really freaked out.

If for some reason the exposure is much harder than you thought it would be and you choose to escape, allow yourself to calm down and use your coping skills. However, it's very important to go back and try again. Also, if you accidentally (or intentionally) use a safety behavior, you should practice the exposure again without the safety behavior. This may mean taking a step back and doing an exposure you are able to complete successfully. Whenever possible, you always want to end your practice with a true exposure, not an escape.

People frequently ask how often they need to practice exposures. The simple answer is as much as possible. Like most skills, the more you practice, the easier it will get. You should practice the same step repeatedly until you feel like you're ready to move on to the next step. Depending on your schedule and the type of experiment you are doing, it could be several times a day or a few times a week. Just remember, the more you practice, the sooner you'll reach your goal.

People also adjust at different rates. Some can practice a step two or three times, and others may need eight to ten times before they are ready to move on. There is no right or wrong number. Some people will notice a big decrease in their fear level during one exposure practice, while others might not notice a difference until they practice the same exposure several times. Overall, try to be realistic about your progress, remembering it will take some time for your brain and body to make changes.

You should also practice in as many different ways as possible. Your brain will need variety in order to generalize your learning. If you practice with only one dog or one elevator, you might not be prepared to handle different dogs or elevators. Mix it up. Be creative and see how many different kinds of experiences you can have.

Draw Conclusions

You did it! Congratulations! You brought all your skills together and took a big step toward conquering your phobia. There are still a few things you need to do after each exposure experiment. Now that you have actually faced your phobia, you have some evidence to support or reject your hypothesis. Think back to what happened during your experiment and see what you can learn from it.

What was your hypothesis? _____

_____

What was your experiment? _____

_____

What did you learn from your experiment? _____

_____

_____

Based on this experiment, do you think your hypothesis is true or false? Why?

_____

_____

_____

Does your new learning support your phobic thoughts or your smart thoughts? Why?

_____

_____

_____

What did you learn about your ability to tolerate discomfort?

_____

_____

_____

What did you learn about the need for safety behaviors?

_____

_____

_____

What do you think you should try next? _____

_____

_____

Reward Yourself

You've done so much hard work, so be sure to celebrate. Give yourself credit for what you just accomplished. Don't fall into the trap of self-criticism or not feeling good enough. Whether what you just took was a first step, a baby step, or a big step, reward yourself. You can even use rewards as motivation, so you have something to look forward to after your exposures. Choose rewards that make you feel happy or relaxed. Rewards can be objects (like a game or ice cream) or experiences (like going to a movie or out to dinner). They should also be special, not things you already do every day. Reward yourself as soon as possible; don't wait!

List some rewards you could earn: _____

_____

_____

_____

_____

_____

_____

_____

Frequently Asked Questions

As you practice your exposure experiments, you might come across some situations you aren't exactly sure how to handle. You are not the only one. Sometimes figuring out the best way to move forward is tricky. The responses to these questions may help answer some of your own questions.

It's hard to find time to practice my exposure experiments. What should I do?

This is a very common problem. Sometimes people are ready to experiment, but with their busy schedules, they struggle to find the time to do it or just plain forget. You may have gone through all the planning steps to prepare for your experiment, but didn't really think about when it would actually happen.

To increase the chance that you can find time or remember to practice, you'll have to do some more planning. Sit down at least one day a week and decide what your exposure plan will be for the rest of the week. Make a very specific plan for which exposures you'll practice and when. This might mean reserving an hour each day in your schedule or planning three or four specific times to practice. Put these times in your calendar and set reminder alarms on your phone. Protect this time, and don't schedule other activities during it.

It's very easy to let other things in your life take over, but you have to remember your values and priorities. Don't let excuses keep you from your goals. If you aren't able to do an experiment because of things you can't control (like you were supposed to practice snorkeling, but it's storming outside), find another way to practice. You have to make it happen! If you just can't get yourself to find the time, you might have to go back to chapter 5 and really consider how motivated you are to make changes at this time.

My experiments have been really easy. Am I doing it right?

This is a great question. When we do exposure experiments, we expect there to be some discomfort or anxiety. In fact, we *want* there to be some level of fear or difficulty; otherwise, it's not really an exposure. If you aren't experiencing discomfort when you practice, it's possible something was missed. Maybe the step you're practicing is just too easy. You can go to the next item on your list and see if that step brings on more emotion. If it does, celebrate that your first steps were easier than you thought they would be and move on with your list.

You also have to consider what else might be making it easy. Sometimes people realize they're using safety behaviors during their experiments. It may even be something you never thought of as a safety behavior until now. Look out for anything you might be leaning on to make the exposure easier, then try it again without that behavior. For example:

Raj practiced watching videos of people getting shots. It was easier than he thought it would be. However, after practicing for a few days, he realized he always looked away right before the shot was given. He never saw the shot happen, so he wasn't actually exposing himself at all. Once he opened his eyes and watched the whole video, the experiment was a little more challenging, but he was able to practice his skills the right way.

The same way you might miss a safety behavior, you also might miss an important variable. There could be one little thing that makes a situation a bit easier or harder. For example:

Adele practiced counting to ten instead of twelve when she had an urge. She realized counting to ten was actually not hard at all because it was another even number. To her, all even numbers acted in the same way and could keep bad things from happening. But she didn't know that at first. To make it a true exposure, she counted to nine instead of ten.

You have to ask yourself what you can do differently to make the exposure more difficult. The goal is to make the experiments challenging, but not impossible.

I know I'm supposed to stay in my exposure until I can naturally adjust, but my experiment doesn't take very long at all. What should I do?

If at all possible, try to make it longer. You want to give your brain and body some time to learn and adjust. It's hard to do this if you practice for only a minute and then stop. To make your exposure longer, you can repeat it several times in a row or even combine a few shorter exposures into a longer one.

For example, it takes only about a minute to ride an elevator, and then you would normally get out. To prolong this exposure, you could ride the elevator, get out, then ride it to another floor, get out, and continue to repeat this process. Or you could stay in the elevator and keep riding it up and down wherever it goes. Remember, exposures aren't necessarily what you would normally do; they are doing everything you can to conquer your fear.

I planned to do my experiment, but when I tried I was just too scared. Now what?

First, take a step back. Review your smart, scientific thoughts and your coping skills. You might also look back at your values and goals to help with motivation. Then go back to the planning stage of your experiment. See if there is an easier step you could possibly take first, or maybe a part of the experiment you could change to make it a bit simpler. It's perfectly okay for your first step to be pretty easy; it's still a success. If you previously used a lot of safety behaviors, you may also need to reduce your safety behaviors gradually. You may not be able to totally stop using them right away. If you usually use three safety behaviors, try using only two. Make sure to plan an experiment that seems possible, knowing you'll work your way up to the harder stuff when you're ready.

Even though your exposure experiments are very similar to the situations you fear in real life, there are some differences. When we interact with our phobias in everyday life, the interactions are usually forced or unexpected. Exposure experiments are the exact opposite. They are strategically planned, and you get to decide what you'll be doing. Exposures are meant to feel more controlled than real life so you can learn from them. Although no one can promise you what will happen when you do an exposure (just like real life), you get to determine your pace and willingness to practice.

Why doesn't my fear level go down when I practice exposures?

There are several reasons this could happen. In order for your brain and body to adjust, you have to give yourself time, so try to be patient. It's possible you need to stay with the exposure longer, even for a few hours. Everyone is different, and your body might need more time to adjust. You've also learned that some people adjust really quickly, while others may need many repetitions. If this is the case, you'll need to practice the exposure more, limiting the amount of time between practice sessions. For example, if you have been practicing for thirty minutes once a week, you could move to practicing thirty minutes every day.

Again, you have to make sure you are not using safety behaviors. Safety behaviors don't allow your brain and body to learn and adjust. They make you feel better in the moment, but your fear level will stay the same over time. Additionally, if phobic thought patterns are taking over during exposures, sometimes they can win. You have to continue to challenge these thoughts.

The good news is, even if your fear level is not going down as quickly as you hoped, you can still overcome your phobia. Many people conquer their phobias by facing them, despite their fear and discomfort. They learn to accept and tolerate the feelings, and not let them get in their way. Think of how many people get really nervous when they speak in public but do it anyway. Think of how many people are afraid of flying but do it anyway. You can let your values and goals, rather than your feelings, lead your life.

What I feared would happen actually happened, and now I'm more scared. What should I do?

It's true; you are taking a risk when you do exposure experiments. No one can promise you that nothing bad will happen or that there will be no consequences, just like in real life. Even really rare things happen sometimes. But go back to your smart, flexible thinking. How can you think about what happened? Did the exposure exercises cause this thing to happen? Are they really related? Even though something you feared actually happened, what did you learn? Was it as bad as you thought it would be? Did you get through it?

Even though it was really scary, now is the time to show your courage and resiliency. Bad things may happen, and you can bounce back. The longer you avoid your fear or turn back to old behaviors, the harder it will be to get back on track. Cowboy wisdom says that you have to get back on the horse that threw you. Cowboys learned that the only way to conquer their fear was to be brave, jump back in, and show the fear who was boss.

With all this information, you can consider yourself an exposure expert. You probably didn't even know what exposures were a few weeks ago, and now you know how to plan exposure experiments, put them into practice, and troubleshoot any problems you might have along the way. Over the next few weeks, make a commitment to practice your new skills and exposures. Put in the time and effort. Your hard work will pay off. And don't forget to come back to the last chapter. You'll learn how to maintain the progress you have made and keep your phobias away for good.

Chapter 10

Keep It Up

The brave man is not he who does not feel afraid, but he who conquers that fear.

—Nelson Mandela, former president of South Africa

You've put a lot of time and energy into conquering your phobia. You've worked hard, challenged yourself, and tolerated discomfort. Hopefully, you've taken the opportunity to enjoy your success. But don't you also want to make sure it lasts? In this chapter, you'll learn how to continue to beat your phobia even when it tries to creep back in and pull you back down.

Where to Go from Here

Think back to when you started reading this book. How were you feeling when you decided it was time to do something about your fear or phobia? What made you want to conquer your fear? Take a few minutes to remember your previous relationship with your phobia.

How was your phobia interfering with your life before you started to conquer it?

_____

_____

_____

_____

_____

Now think about all the steps you have taken to face your phobia. What progress have you made toward conquering it?

_____

_____

_____

_____

Remember to give yourself credit for your successes, whether your changes have been big or small. To keep moving in the right direction, you have to decide what to do next.

After reflecting on your progress, what is your next step?

☐ I definitely challenged myself and made a lot of progress. I just need to keep doing what I'm doing.

☐ The skills I've learned make sense, but I probably need to go back and really put them into daily practice.

☐ I'm not sure I was really invested in learning and practicing skills. I might have to come back to the book later when I'm more ready for change.

☐ I gave it a really good effort, but I'm still not where I want to be. Maybe I need to look for some extra help from a coach or therapist.

All these steps are great. It's important to be honest with yourself about your progress. At the same time, you have to be realistic about how much change is actually possible. If your idea of progress is to never feel fear again, you'll definitely be disappointed and feel like you have not reached your goal. Even once you've conquered your phobia, you'll still feel fear. Remember, fear is a basic human emotion that is necessary for survival. If your goal is not to have fear, it's like you're saying your goal is not to be human. What you *can* achieve is learning how to manage your fear and anxiety when it arrives and not let it spiral out of control.

Sneaky Phobias

No one likes to be pushed to the side. Think of your phobia as a really annoying little pest. Most pests don't give up easily. They keep trying and trying, hoping that sooner or later they will wear you down. The good news is, you found a way to win! Your phobia had to surrender, admit defeat, and move to the sidelines. But at some point, it might just try again. After some time, pests look for breaks, cracks, and vulnerabilities. They look for any situation that could provide an opportunity to jump back in. Here are some situations where your phobia might try to take advantage of you. So look out.

Overconfidence

Jeff was feeling really good. With hard work and persistence, he was able to conquer his fear of being outside by himself. The last exposure on his checklist was to spend the night in a tent in his backyard. He did it all by himself without going inside or asking his parents for help or reassurance. Since Jeff's checklist was completed, he thought he was done. He had beaten his fear, so there was nothing left for him to do. Right?

Unfortunately, when he went to summer camp a year later, he realized his fear had come back. He had not practiced his brave behaviors for almost a year, and he forgot what to do. Jeff wasn't prepared. His progress and overconfidence led him to believe he no longer needed to practice or challenge his fear. As a result, his phobia found a way in and returned.

Early Contentment

Henry was doing a good job completing his exposure experiments. In order to face his germ phobia, he practiced touching money with his hands rather than with gloves. He was successful and could now pay for things without needing his gloves. But once he got to harder steps on his checklist, he decided he was happy with his progress and didn't want to go any further. He was sick of doing exposures and thought he had done enough.

While everyone has the right to decide how far they want to go with their exposures, it's important to know the possible outcomes. Henry didn't complete all the experiments on his list, which meant there were still some areas where his phobia was in charge. Even so, Henry became satisfied with the quality of his life. Sure, there were some limitations and minor fears, but he felt okay. However, stopping halfway left the door open for a very unwelcome guest.

The Unexpected

Nora completed her checklist and continued to practice her exposures related to riding on the subway. She even went above and beyond and rode the subway for a whole day. Through this practice she learned she could tolerate the discomfort of small, crowded spaces. She was feeling really good about her progress, until one day when the subway got stuck. Her worst-case scenario actually happened.

This is an amazing opportunity for a phobia. If Nora lets her phobia creep back, she will likely find herself going back to her rigid thought patterns and safety behaviors, just in case. She might also take this rare occurrence and start to see it as highly likely again. Rather than focusing on the fact that she made it through her worst-case scenario, her phobia will push her to focus only on how bad it felt.

Stress

Emma made it to the point where she no longer requires her boyfriend to promise her that she doesn't have cancer. She exposed herself to situations she would have normally avoided, like sitting in the sun, eating more meat, and putting her cell phone next to her ear (all of which she thinks will give her cancer). Emma enjoyed a pretty relaxing summer and is in the third week of her senior year of high school. She's taking four AP classes, and the amount of homework is way more than she thought it would be. She has no idea how she's going to catch up. And to add to her stress, her worry about cancer is increasing again.

When stress or other negative events happen in our lives, our phobias see vulnerability. Our defenses are down. We're caught up in other things and are not focusing our time and attention on keeping our phobias away. Phobias can be bullies and kick us when we're down.

If you know your phobia's sneaky tricks, you know what to look out for. It's very easy to fall back into old habits if we aren't careful.

How do you think your phobia might try to find its way back in?

_____

_____

_____

What If I Slip?

Even if you are really good about filling the cracks, the pest might still get in. In the same way, even if you practice your skills and challenge your phobia, it might sneak in. But that's okay. You are human. We all slip or fall back into old habits every once in a while. Think about other skills you might have learned. Just because you're good at making three-point shots in basketball or getting strikes in bowling does not necessarily mean you'll get one every time. Just because you learned how to bake really good pies or paint amazing art pieces doesn't mean they'll be perfect. The truth is, you might slip. It happens. For example:

When Toby started facing his fears, he made a game out of it. Every day, he challenged his phobia in some way. Toby used to repeat simple tasks over and over until they felt right, and he asked his parents for a lot of reassurance. Most of his experiments included doing a task, like closing a door or washing the dishes, only once. He pretended there was a time clock counting down, so he had to do it really quickly and could not ask for reassurance. After he completed a challenge, he marked a point on a homemade scoreboard, which showed Toby had 25 points and "The Gremlins" (which he named his phobia) had 0. But one day, he accidentally used a safety behavior. Instead of quickly walking out the door without questions, he asked his dad for reassurance. Toby was so mad at himself. He immediately went to his scoreboard and erased all his points.

Why do you think Toby erased all his points? _____

_____

What do you think he should have done instead? _____

_____

At times, you might use a safety behavior or get stuck in phobic thoughts. But this is not a disaster. It doesn't mean you failed or lost all your progress. It just means there was a bump in the road. Do drivers who get flat tires just leave their cars and give up? No, they fix the tires and keep going.

Instead of getting mad at ourselves, we have to accept that there are ups and downs when we grow and change. You can use the downs as learning experiences, just like any slip or mistake. You can even thank your phobia for pointing out where you might need a little more practice. Maybe you need to try a new exposure or challenge a new thought that crept in.

A slip *does not* mean you are starting from the beginning, because you still have all your new learning and skills. Every day you conquer your phobia is a positive one, and nothing can take that away from you. A slip *does* mean it's time to keep practicing and being brave. And the quicker you can get back to it, the better. Don't let one slip pull you down.

Stay in Charge

Once you have made some progress with your phobia, there are a few things you can do to stay on track.

1. Know what works.

   Think about how you made progress. What made you successful? What skills did you use to conquer your phobia? If you know how you were able to make positive changes, then you know what you should keep doing. List what worked for you:

   _____

   _____

   _____

2. Be proactive.

   Don't wait around for your phobia to try to sneak back in. Be a few steps ahead. If you actively challenge yourself and practice your skills on a regular basis, you won't be caught off guard.

3. Make exposure part of your regular routine.

   Don't stop experimenting. Find a way to practice your exposures as often as you can. Be creative and continue to approach your phobia as much as possible, even when you feel like everything is going really well.

4. Check in with yourself.

   Every few weeks, take some time to sit down and think about your progress. You can even go through your list of skills and give yourself a grade. Think about how often you are practicing. Check for any safety behaviors or phobic thoughts that need to be challenged. And make a plan for the following weeks.

Celebrate Your Success

You've come so far! Celebrate your effort and accomplishments. Sometimes people forget to take the time to congratulate themselves and to actually get excited about what they have done.

What things have you done that you never thought you could?

_____

_____

_____

_____

What goals have you accomplished? _____

_____

_____

_____

By working to conquer your phobia, what values have you followed?

_____

_____

_____

_____

How do you feel about yourself? _____

_____

_____

_____

How will conquering your phobia affect your future? _____

_____

_____

_____

How will you reward yourself for your accomplishments?

_____

_____

_____

_____

The steps you've taken are important not only for conquering your phobia, but also for facing any obstacles in your life. Your commitment, willingness, and courage will continue to help you face many different kinds of challenges. You are strong. You are capable. And you are brave.

Answers

Chapter 1
Fear and Your Body

1–e; 2–c; 3–h; 4–g; 5–d; 6–b; 7–f; 8–a; 9–i

Real Threat vs. False Alarm

Situation	Real Threat (Bear)	False Alarm (Squirrel)
A bat is flying around Mia's house and might have already bitten her.	X	
Kristi is eating greasy food and feels like she might throw up.		X
An ant crawls onto Mark's arm.		X
Jorden sees an electrical line down in her front yard.	X	
Trey falls off his skateboard and breaks his arm.	X	
Sasha is afraid of getting into an accident while driving.		X
An older boy hits Caleb in the hallway.	X	
Jacob gets a head rush when he goes down the waterslide.		X
Josh's friend shows him his loaded gun.	X	
Ella is choking on a piece of food.	X	
Craig thinks the elevator might get stuck.		X
Tammy hates getting shots, and it's time for her flu shot.		X

Chapter 2
Putting the Pieces Together

Possible Factors	Betsy's Phobia Factors
Genetically inherited	Betsy's mother seems like an anxious person, especially around driving, so Betsy probably inherited some anxiety from her mother.
Direct negative association	Betsy was in an accident when she was young but does not seem to remember it.
Observation and learning	Betsy's mother holds on tight. She is also teaching Betsy to look for ways to escape and to drive in the right lane at all times. Betsy also went to the funeral of two classmates who died in an accident.
Information	Betsy's teacher warned the class about teen accident and death rates. Her mother also seems to be giving lots of warnings.
Amount of experience	Betsy has never driven a motorized vehicle before so she has no experience driving. However, she probably has a lot of experience riding in a vehicle.
Level of stress	We don't have a lot of information about her stress level.

Possible Factors	Alex's Phobia Factors
Genetically inherited	We don't much have information about Alex's family, so this may or may not be a factor.
Direct negative association	Alex became frightened when watching the movie, and he associated this with darkness.
Observation and learning	Alex observed bad things happening to people in the movie.
Information	Alex learned about the kidnapping. Even though this incident happened in 1932 and kidnapping is very rare in general, it still scared him.
Amount of experience	It's likely that Alex has not seen a lot of scary movies before.
Level of stress	Alex could have some stress related to having a new baby brother in the house.

Chapter 3
Thought or Emotion?

Statement	Thought	Emotion
I'm worried about throwing up.		X
My plane is going to crash.	X	
I'll never be able to go outside again.	X	
I'm frustrated that I cannot do this perfectly.		X
A really big thunderstorm is coming.	X	
I'm so mad that my mom made me go to the doctor.		X
When I eat greasy food, I get really sick.	X	
I know that dog is going to hurt me.	X	
I love spending time with my friends.		X
Being in the dark scares me.		X

Identifying the Spiraling STAIRS in Others

Nicole's initial trigger: Hearing about a plane crash on the news

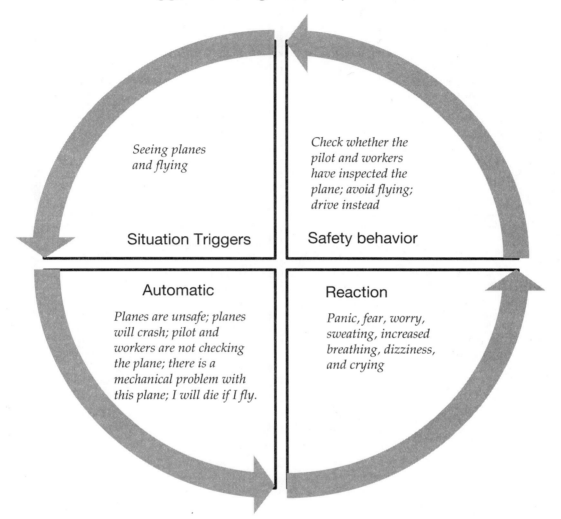

Situation Triggers

Seeing planes and flying

Safety behavior

Check whether the pilot and workers have inspected the plane; avoid flying; drive instead

Automatic

Planes are unsafe; planes will crash; pilot and workers are not checking the plane; there is a mechanical problem with this plane; I will die if I fly.

Reaction

Panic, fear, worry, sweating, increased breathing, dizziness, and crying

Logan's initial trigger: Dad's heart attack

Situation Triggers

Running in soccer game and heart beating fast

Safety behavior

Get out of the game and avoid activities that will increase heart rate

Automatic Interpretation

I'm going to have a heart attack; my heart is not strong enough; my dad had a heart attack and so will I.

Reaction

Panic, fear, heavy breathing, shaking, and heart beating even faster

Chapter 4
Practice Breaking Phobia Patterns

Parts of the Phobia Pattern	Lily's Phobia Pattern	Possible FACE Strategies
Situation triggers	Blood, anything that looks like blood, red liquids, thoughts about blood Most recent: Elena's nosebleed	Help her recognize she can't completely control her environment. The situation isn't the problem; the fear is.
Automatic interpretations	Blood is associated with pain or something bad happening	Flexible Thinking: not all blood means horrible pain; people can tolerate pain; bleeding is temporary; there aren't always terrible consequences; it's usually a false alarm.
Reactions	Lightheaded, dizzy, sweaty, fast heart rate, crying, creeped out, afraid, guilty	Acceptance and Coping: her body reacts when she's scared; she can tolerate uncomfortable feelings; these feelings are temporary.
Safety behaviors	Don't look at the blood; don't play sports or go to sporting events; avoid the doctor; avoid red liquids; avoid people who might have nosebleeds.	Coping and Exposure: slowly learn to face blood, taking it one step at a time, as a long-term fix rather than a short-term fix; she can challenge herself and do hard things.

Chapter 6
Phobic Thought Traps

Camilla

Predicting the negative: *If I got on that train, I knew it would get stuck.*

Generalizing: *The subway got stuck last time, so it will get stuck this time, too.*

Exaggerating the severity: *It was not going to be fine. It was terrifying. We're going to get stuck forever. No one will find us for hours.*

Demanding certainty: *I would rather take a taxi; it seems like a safer option. There is no way I was doing that again. There is no way I'm letting that happen.*

Underestimating abilities: *I would freak out.*

Victor

Demanding certainty: *I couldn't get past not knowing what was in there and not being able to see at all. I just kept thinking that I had no idea what was in that water.*

Underestimating abilities: *The muddy water was just too much. I couldn't make myself do it.*

Choosing a Path

Thoughts	Path 1: Haunted House (Phobia)	Path 2: Scientific (Smart Brain)
The likelihood that this is an ulcer is probably low.		X
I'll never be able to get this job, or any job.	X	
There is something wrong with me.	X	
My stomach might hurt because I'm nervous about the interview.		X
I need to go to the doctor now.	X	
I'm going to die.	X	
I've had stomachaches before and it wasn't an ulcer.		X
I ate really greasy food last night.		X
I can get through this.		X

Chapter 7
Balance Your Emotions

R = reasoning mind   E = emotional mind   W = wise mind

R Sherlock Holmes

E Dr. John Watson

R Bill Gates

W Superman

R Dr. Who

R Sheldon (from *The Big Bang Theory*)

E Miley Cyrus

E Homer Simpson

W Dalai Lama

R Hermione Granger (from the Harry Potter series)

E Ron Weasley (from the Harry Potter series)

W Dumbledore (from the Harry Potter series)

W Professor Xavier (from the X-Men series)

E Wolverine (from the X-Men series)

E The Hulk

E Kim Kardashian

E Kirk (from the Star Trek series)

R Spock (from the Star Trek series)

W Yoda (from the Star Wars series)

R C3PO (from the Star Wars series)

E Han Solo (from the Star Wars series)

R Mark Zuckerberg

E Justin Bieber

Additional Resources

For Teens: Phobias

Antony, Martin, and Randi McCabe. *Overcoming Animal and Insect Phobias: How to Conquer Fear of Dogs, Snakes, Rodents, Bees, Spiders, and More.* Oakland, CA: New Harbinger Publications, 2005.

Antony, Martin, and Karen Rowa. *Overcoming Fear of Heights: How to Conquer Acrophobia and Live a Life Without Limits.* Oakland, CA: New Harbinger Publications, 2007.

Antony, Martin, and Mark Watling. *Overcoming Medical Phobias: How to Conquer Fear of Blood, Needles, Doctors, and Dentists.* Oakland, CA: New Harbinger Publications, 2006.

Greenberg, Gary, and Matthew Reinhart. *The Pop-Up Book of Phobias.* New York, NY: Rob Weisbach Books at William Morrow, 1999.

Latta, Sara. *Scared Stiff: Everything You Need to Know About 50 Famous Phobias.* San Francisco, CA: Zest Books, 2014.

For Teens: Anxiety

Fox, Marci, and Leslie Sokol. *Think Confident, Be Confident for Teens: A Cognitive Therapy Guide to Overcoming Self-Doubt and Creating Unshakable Self-Esteem.* Oakland, CA: New Harbinger Publications, 2011.

Greenspon, Thomas. *What to Do When Good Enough Isn't Good Enough: The Real Deal on Perfectionism.* Minneapolis, MN: Free Spirit Publishing, 2007.

Munroe, Erin. *The Anxiety Workbook for Girls.* Minneapolis, MN: Fairview Press, 2010.

Tompkins, Michael, and Katherine Martinez. *My Anxious Mind: A Teen's Guide to Managing Anxiety and Panic.* Washington, DC: Magination Press, 2009.

Wilson, Reid, and Lynn Lyons. *Playing with Anxiety: Casey's Guide for Teens and Kids.* Chapel Hill, NC: Pathway Systems, 2014.

For Parents

Albano, Anne Marie, and Leslie Pepper. *You and Your Anxious Child: Free Your Child from Fears and Worries and Create a Joyful Family Life.* New York, NY: Penguin Group, 2013.

Chansky, Tamar. *Freeing Your Child from Anxiety: Powerful, Practical Solutions to Overcome Your Child's Fears, Worries, and Phobias.* New York, NY: Harmony Books, 2014.

Foa, Edna, and Linda Wasmer Andrews. *If Your Adolescent Has an Anxiety Disorder: An Essential Resource for Parents.* New York, NY: Oxford University Press, 2006.

Pinto Wagner, Aureen. *Worried No More: Help and Hope for Anxious Children.* Apex, NC: Lighthouse Press, 2005.

Tolin, David. *Face Your Fears: A Proven Plan to Beat Anxiety, Panic, Phobias, and Obsessions.* Hoboken, NJ: John Wiley & Sons, 2012.

Wilson, Reid, and Lynn Lyons. *Anxious Kids, Anxious Parents: 7 Ways to Stop the Worry Cycle and Raise Courageous and Independent Children.* Deerfield Beach, FL: Health Communications, 2013.

Informational Websites

Dr. Andrea Umbach: http://www.drandreaumbach.com

Southeast Psych: http://www.southeastpsych.com

Anxiety and Depression Association of America (ADAA): http://www.adaa.org

Association for Behavioral and Cognitive Therapies (ABCT): http://www.abct.org

International OCD Foundation (IOCDF): http://www.ocfoundation.org

American Psychological Association (APA): http://www.apa.org

Anxieties.com: http://www.anxieties.com

References

American Psychiatric Association. 2013. *Diagnostic and Statistical Manual of Mental Disorders* (5th ed.). Washington, DC: American Psychological Association.

Kessler, R. C., P. Berglund, O. Demler, R. Jin, K. R. Merikangas, and E. E. Walters. 2005. "Lifetime Prevalence and Age-of-Onset Distributions of DSM-IV Disorders in the National Comorbidity Survey Replication." *Archives of General Psychiatry* 62: 593–602.

Linehan, M. 1993. *Cognitive-Behavioral Treatment of Borderline Personality Disorder.* New York: The Guilford Press.

Merikangas, K. R., J. He, M. Burstein, S. A. Swanson, S. Avenevoli, L. Cui, C. Benjet, K. Georgiades, and J. Swendsen. 2010. "Lifetime Prevalence of Mental Disorders in U.S. Adolescents: Results from the National Comorbidity Survey Replication-Adolescent Supplement (NCS-A)." *Journal of the American Academy of Child & Adolescent Psychiatry* 49: 980–989.

Prochaska, J. O., & DiClemente, C. C. 1982. "Transtheoretical Therapy: Toward a More Integrative Model of Change." *Psychotherapy: Theory, Research, and Practice* 19(3): 276–88.

Quiodbach, J., D. T. Gilbert, and T. D. Wilson. "The End of History Illusion." *Science* 339: 96–98.

Rachman, S. 1977. "The Conditioning Theory of Fear-Acquisition: A Critical Examination." *Behaviour Research and Therapy* 15: 375–387.

Rachman, S. 1976. "The Passing of the Two-Stage Theory of Fear and Avoidance: Fresh Possibilities." *Behaviour Research and Therapy* 14: 125–131.

U.S. Geological Survey. 2014. "Earthquake Hazards Program." Retrieved from http://earthquake.usgs.gov

Andrea Umbach, PsyD, is a clinical psychologist and anxiety expert who is passionate about helping individuals face and overcome their fears in order to allow for more functional and anxiety-free living. Umbach has trained under experts in the areas of anxiety, hoarding, and trichotillomania. She practices from a cognitive behavioral approach focused on increasing flexibility in thinking and making adaptive behavior changes. Umbach enjoys working with kids, teens, and adults in both individual and group formats, and provides trainings, presentations, and consultations. Visit her online at http://www.drandreaumbach.com and http://southeastpsych.com.

More Instant Help Books for Teens

An Imprint of New Harbinger Publications

Register your **new harbinger** titles for additional benefits!

When you register your **new harbinger** title—purchased in any format, from any source—you get access to benefits like the following:

- Downloadable accessories like printable worksheets and extra content
- Instructional videos and audio files
- Information about updates, corrections, and new editions

Not every title has accessories, but we're adding new material all the time.

Access free accessories in 3 easy steps:

1. Sign in at NewHarbinger.com (or **register** to create an account).

2. Click on **register a book**. Search for your title and click the **register** button when it appears.

3. Click on the **book cover or title** to go to its details page. Click on **accessories** to view and access files.

That's all there is to it!

If you need help, visit:

NewHarbinger.com/accessories

new harbinger
CELEBRATING
40 YEARS